WANTED

DEAD & ALIVE

WANTED

DEAD & ALIVE

GREGORY MTHEMBU-SALTER

face2face

First published in 2019 by Face2Face
an imprint of Cover2Cover books

www.cover2cover.co.za

© Gregory Mthembu-Salter

ISBN: 978-1-928466-13-0
e-ISBN: 978-1-928466-14-7

Cover designer: Publicide
Book designer: Pete Bosman
Editors: Jennifer Stastny (Clarity Editorial, Cape Town) and Mandi Smallhorne
Indexer: Natasha Ndlebe (Clarity Editorial, Cape Town)
Proofreading: Inga Norenius

CONTENTS

FOREWORD

We live in an age of rapid expansion in knowledge production and the proliferation of provocative questions about our way of life and our interaction with the environment that we share with nature's diverse abundance.

Through the course of numerous centuries, South Africa's first nations and modern society have come to form cultural and economic attachments to *cattle* as an indicator of social and financial standing; as matrimonial currency; as inspiration and material content for creative industries; and as the *raison d'être* for keeping our braai stands and stoves on the boil.

The history of cattle in our country is indeed the history of pre-colonial freedom; of colonial and apartheid dispossession and our present-day endeavours to return people to the land and satisfy our hunger for and love of the land and its bounty.

With *Wanted Dead & Alive: The Case for South Africa's Cattle*, Gregory Mthembu-Salter celebrates our national affinity for cattle and disrupts our under-appreciation or outright ignorance of food consumption patterns and cattle farming practices that hold grave implications for our physical environment.

This is an environment which, if not managed sustainably and humanely, will endanger human existence as well as the future of the very cattle that are the centrepiece of social interaction, physical sustenance and economic value chains.

The author challenges us to find it within ourselves to reimagine life alongside cattle; life where we change our behaviour in ways that will reduce our reliance on mass-produced beef, the production of which carries enormous environmental impacts in South Africa and globally.

Passionately and colourfully, Gregory Mthembu-Salter walks us through history and causes us to look at our future differently, perching us uncomfortably on the horns of multiple dilemmas.

In a nation that thrives on debate and where we have more opinions than heads of cattle, this book will keep us talking and hopefully inspire action towards a better future for humans and herds alike.

Mr Matamela Cyril Ramaphosa
President of the Republic of South Africa
16 July 2019

Braai nation under attack

*It was my very first memory, a magnificent parade
of dark shapes shifting against a red sky. I remember
hearing the bellowing of the bulls, the cry of young
voices who say kumpondozankomo? It is the time of
the horns of the cattle. It is the dawn, my brothers ...*

HEAVEN'S HERDS (2006 FILM DIRECTED BY SOFIA DE FAY AND JAMES HERSOV)

South Africans love their cattle, dead and alive. They may be
commercially farmed or part of a small and cherished family herd.
They may be lined up for lobola, milked for amasi or meet their end
as choice cuts on the braai. But the love is there. South Africa is still
the braai nation.

This book traces the national cattle hunger, a hunger that extends
far back in time and traverses the whole country, exploring its meaning
and whether it can still be justified in an era increasingly dominated
by the worsening effects of climate breakdown.

In June 2018, *The Guardian* newspaper published an article under
the headline: 'The best way to save the planet? Drop the meat and
dairy'. In it, British environmental writer George Monbiot wrote:

All the evidence now points in one direction: the crucial shift is
from an animal- to a plant-based diet ... While some kinds of
meat and dairy production are more damaging than others, all

1

are more harmful to the living world than growing plant protein … Animal farming takes up 83% of the world's agricultural land but delivers only 18% of our calories. A plant-based diet cuts the use of land by 76% and halves the greenhouse gases and other pollution that are caused by food production.

How does it happen? How has farming livestock come to take up so much land and contribute so much to global warming or, more accurately, global heating? The answer lies in the way commercial livestock is currently farmed. *Grazed and Confused?*, a 2017 report by the University of Oxford's Food Climate Research Network (FCRN), cites Brazil as an example of how poor livestock management by commercial farmers is directly accelerating climate breakdown. Here, huge swathes of the Amazon rainforest – a vital carbon sink – are being cleared to make way for cattle ranches and enormous soy plantations, with much of this soy subsequently being used to feed livestock.

Disasters like this support Monbiot's view that the world should, urgently and entirely, dispense with livestock farming. To make up for the loss of meat in the human diet, the large percentage of crops that currently ends up as animal fodder could simply be eaten by humans instead. The newly derelict pastures can then, Monbiot says, be rewilded, returned to their natural state. Where crops are still grown, the focus should be on plant-based composts and plants that replenish the nitrogen in soils depleted by food crops.

In South Africa, phasing out all livestock farming would mean not only goodbye to our cattle, but also to sheep, goat, donkeys and horses. It would have a significant and, for many, a devastating impact. Given this effect, we would need to be absolutely sure that there were no alternatives before embarking on such a drastic course. And, as I argue on these pages, there are good South African alternatives.

But before all that, I should explain how my interest in South Africa's relationship with cattle was sparked in the first place.

The inspiration came when I saw the 2006 film *Heaven's Herds*, a beautiful, evocative account of Nguni cattle and the tender place they occupy in the hearts of so many rural households. Leaving the cinema, my wife and I went to a superette for some supplies, where we found ourselves standing in front of a freezer full of beef cuts wrapped in clingfilm and rickety towers of garishly pink polony. The contrast between the supply chains that provide these industrial meat products and the complex, ancient human cultures that still embrace Nguni, as portrayed in the movie, stayed with me, seeming to point to a way for a first-generation, white immigrant like myself to better understand this country.

This quest, to understand the country through the rich and diverse relationships between its people and its cattle, took me on a decade-long journey across southern Africa. Researching for this book, I have had the privilege of speaking to dozens of people from all races, cultures and stations in life. And everyone I spoke to – from the Zulu farmers in rural KwaZulu-Natal to the cattle-herding politicians to the genetics-hunting breeder in Namibia – had an important story to tell that has barely been heard before.

My own cattle story began sometime before that, back in 1995, when my newly appointed umkhongi (negotiator) went to Kwa-Mashu, Durban, to open discussions with negotiators from the family of Lindiwe, my wife-to-be, about the lobola I needed to pay her parents. As Zulu custom requires, the umkhongi delivered a goat to my future in-laws to initiate proceedings, in which it soon became evident that the key issue to resolve was how many cattle I needed to pay upfront, and how much cash.

Zulu culture is adamant that lobola must include cattle – 12 is often said to be the ideal minimum – in part as compensation to the family for the loss of their daughter, and also as a resource for the daughter's use should she ever quit the marriage and return to her parents. This can work against the bride, since sometimes parents refuse to accept their daughter's divorce for fear of having to part with her lobola cattle.

Another reason lobola has to include cattle is the deep link between them and the family ancestors. Without a transfer of cattle between the families, the thinking goes, the ancestors will not have been properly informed of the marriage. And one thing that makes ancestors upset (as is typically true for the living, too), is not being kept informed about what is going on.

These beliefs and practices started when Zulu society was entirely rural but, despite much disruption, urbanisation and industrialisation since, they have been tenaciously retained. Not least among these disruptions has been Christianity, which many understand to oppose the veneration of ancestors (though what, after all, is really so different between an ancestor and a saint, except the Church's blessing on the latter?). A hallmark of Zulu responses to such changes, and the main reason for their retention of these beliefs and practices in spite of them, has been flexibility. In our case, flexibility meant making a plan to cope with the fact that my parents-in-law live in a small township house with no space for a kraal. Also at issue was the cow my in-laws were supposed to supply for an all-night ancestral ceremony on the eve of our wedding day. Whose herd was that going to come from? And who among her family would be fronting the cash for it? In the end, after many umqombothi-lubricated discussions, the pragmatic resolution was that our lobola cow would be the one slaughtered for the all-night ceremony.

That left finding the cow. Had I been Zulu, my father would have selected a choice beast from his herd. If he lacked a herd, he would still have known exactly where else to find the right cow. Instead, ubaba Ntombela, a close and old friend of my wife's family with relatives in the cattle lands of northern KwaZulu-Natal, came to the rescue, finding us a cow that duly arrived on the back of a truck at my parents-in-law's house a few days before the wedding. The cow, light brown and a tad skinny, seemed to sense what was coming, reluctantly descending from the truck only after a couple of whacks to her rump from the driver, and then staying in the corner of the tiny front lawn, tethered to a small tree, disconsolately chewing on the little grass available, while the wedding preparations gathered pace all around her.

The day before the wedding, the early evening air was hot and impossibly humid. Durban style. Ntombela stepped forward and slowly sharpened a long knife. Then, with a large crowd now watching, he walked gently to the cow and swiftly, skilfully, slit her throat. The cow let out a muted bellow and fell to her knees. Thanduxolo, my brother-in-law, darted in with a bucket to collect the blood that spurted from her neck. That done, he and Ntombela immediately began skinning the limp carcass, roping in all the men present during the final stages to hold her hide as they sliced away the meat and muscle.

Next, the meat and intestines were carted off around the back of the house, where my mother-in-law and a small army of female helpers were waiting. The women tipped all the meat into vast iron pots over two open fires, washed the guts of their undigested and semi-digested grass – a messy, intensely aromatic business – and then cooked them, too. Late in the evening, family members gathered in a small side room where a dish of intestines was waiting on a plate as a delicacy for the ancestors. We burned impepho (a yellow 'everlasting' flower of the *Helichrysum* family, widely used in ritual ceremonies) to alert the ancestors that we were seeking to communicate. One after another, everyone said the things they felt they needed to say. New to this, I mumbled something short and let others do the talking.

The hours rolled on. The evening doubled as my stag night, naturally requiring more beer, brewed in vast quantities for the occasion by my mother-in-law. Early the next morning, with many of us feeling much the worse for wear, uMa dished us up distressingly lightly cooked beef kidneys and liver.

The wedding day progressed more smoothly from there on, marred only by a brief mechanical breakdown of the vehicle transporting us to the ceremony, and the minibus taxi tasked with bringing the post-ceremony feast failing to arrive at the wedding venue, necessitating a mad dash back to KwaMashu by my best man to collect it. We learned later that our original driver had been prevailed upon by others to carry a fresh corpse to a morgue. All the beef and much else besides was noisily consumed at the wedding feast, until there was nothing left. The cow's hide and horns stayed with my in-laws, the horns finding their way onto their roof for ancestral reasons, where they sat for many years.

Like the animals themselves, cattle tales often seem to move slowly and widely – embodying in their wandering the essence of a deeper trait or truth. In writing these stories, I have ended up, like my grazing subjects, shifting from one aspect to another: from South Africa's torrid past to its contested present and uncertain future; from lobola to the braai; from trying to understand homesteads where cattle are family to feedlots where they most definitely are not; from ancestors to the Spur; from the apocalyptic cattle killings of old to post-apartheid land reform; and, finally, from an understanding of cattle as methane-emitting climate breakdown culprits to the claim that they can become our soil building, carbon sequestering champions. But before the future, the past. The next chapter looks at some of the episodes in South African history where cattle have played a starring role, beginning thousands of years ago with the Khoekhoe, selectively traversing the vast time span in between, and ending with the present day.

CHAPTER ONE

Cattle in South African history

The relationship between South Africans and their cattle – and between one another over their cattle – is long-running and, at times, epic. It begins not with the nomadic hunter-gathering San, who despite their affinity for the eland over thousands of years never quite got around to domesticating it, but with the Khoekhoe, who moved into the area with their livestock roughly 16 000 years after the San first appeared. (Today, the Khoekhoe and the San are collectively known as the KhoiSan, making moot the question of whether the two are ethnically distinct or, as some maintain, two economic classes of the same ethnic group.)

Until recently, it was thought that the Khoekhoe originally herded sheep, and it was only much later, around AD 650, that the Bantu-speaking agro-pastoralists of the Eastern Cape introduced them to cattle. Disturbing this theory, researchers have since found the remains of *Bos taurus* cattle at two sites in Namaqualand, close to the Western Cape's Atlantic coast. These remains date from between AD 421 and AD 559 – well before Bantu-speaking agro-pastoralists would have reached the Cape. No one quite knows exactly how these cattle made their way to Namaqualand.

The *Bos taurus* cattle of the Khoekhoe and the Bantu-speaking agro-pastoralists were descended, as are all cattle, from *Bos taurus primigenius*, the legendary auroch. Two main lines of domesticated cattle have come from the auroch: *Bos taurus* and *Bos indicus*.

Bos indicus, also known as the Zebu, is distinguished by its hump and short horns. The Zebu was domesticated in the Indus valley around 5000 BC, and later introduced to Africa through what are today Egypt, Sudan and South Sudan. Most African cattle, however, derive from *Bos taurus*, though often with a significant Zebu influence. Sometimes, as with the Nguni, the Zebu influence is dominant.

Of European explorers and Khoekhoe cattle

In 1488, Bartolomeu Dias, a gentleman of the court of the Portuguese monarch Afonso V, became the first outsider to round the Cape by ship. Dias reported seeing Khoekhoe and their cattle on the shore there, but the ship's appearance alarmed the Khoekhoe and they disappeared inland, driving their cattle before them. The Portuguese continued east along the coast, finally landing at Mossel Bay, where they took on fresh water. Dias' sailors fought the Khoekhoe they encountered there, killing one with a crossbow.

Dias went home soon after, apparently at his crew's insistence, and brought back the news that the Cape was green and fertile, and that its people had sheep and cattle in plenty – but had not been friendly. No further expeditions were made for a decade, until Vasco da Gama rounded the Cape in November 1497. Da Gama landed, as had Dias, at Mossel Bay, only he bore gifts. These the Khoekhoe accepted while the Portuguese sailors were still coming onto shore. Emboldened, the Portuguese gave bracelets to the Khoekhoe in return for a large black ox.

After Da Gama and his men had been there two weeks, a Khoekhoe delegation arrived and started shouting at them, evidently displeased, before driving their cattle inland. A nervous Da Gama, sensing trouble, fired a cannon as a show of strength. Nothing happened, and Da Gama sailed on.

Five years later, in 1503, another Portuguese explorer, Antonio de Saldanha, landed and disembarked at Table Bay in what is now the heart of Cape Town. Saldanha climbed up and down Table Mountain and his troops clashed with Khoekhoe herdsmen before he sailed on east. After that, European seafarers left the Cape alone for another 149 years.

Da Gama and other early explorers wrote graphically of the Khoekhoe's strong odour, the result of the latter smearing themselves in lard and wearing sheep and beef intestines as necklaces. The Portuguese, who had been many weeks at sea in outrageously unhygienic conditions, seemed unaware of their own inevitable stench. The resulting mutual, uncomprehending stink-out set the tone for much of what was to come.

The battle for grazing

In February 1656, four years after the Dutch East India Company (technically the Vereenigde Oost-Indische Compagnie, or VOC) settled permanently at the Cape, governor Jan van Riebeeck forbade the Goringhaicona and Goqosoa clans of the Khoekhoe from grazing their cattle in Table Bay because, he claimed, there would be too little grazing left for the VOC's herd.

A year later, Van Riebeeck ordered that the lush valley of the Liesbeek River be divided into farms for the free burghers – people who had been released from service to the VOC to farm food for the growing European settlement. The Liesbeek River flows from the eastern slopes of Table Mountain into what are now the Cape Town suburbs of Newlands, Rondebosch and Observatory, and had, until then, provided rich grazing for the Khoekhoe's cattle. The Khoekhoe resisted, repeatedly attacking settler farmers and plundering their cattle. This prompted the first concerted VOC campaign against the Khoekhoe, led by one Abraham Gabbema in 1657. The skirmishes culminated in the first Khoekhoe-Dutch war of 1660, which went badly for the Khoekhoe and resulted in the VOC annexing all the land from Table Bay to Saldanha Bay, just over 100 km away.

And so a pattern was set. The VOC governor would give land to free burghers. Free burghers would establish farms, booting the Khoekhoe from traditional grazing lands in the process. The Khoekhoe would strike back, and the VOC would organise a military expedition against them in the name of punishing the evil of stock theft. In the process, the VOC would claim more land. First went the Eerste River valley towards Stellenbosch. Then the Hottentots Holland, the Franschhoek and the Drakenstein valleys went to the VOC. Later, in 1700, the Waveren valley, in which the town of Tulbagh now stands, and the area around Riebeek Kasteel were claimed.

The latter annexations were particularly disastrous for the Khoekhoe, who in most cases lost their herds and were forced either to flee and live like the San in the mountains, or seek menial employment with the settlers. Many Khoekhoe who opted for the mountains remained determined, at least initially, to resist the settlers. In the early decades of the 18th century, an undeclared war raged in the Cape as dispossessed Khoekhoe teamed up with San to raid white-owned farms, taking back cattle where they could. Local white farmers formed commandoes to fight back and reclaim their bovine booty, inflicting heavy casualties in the process.

The mass cattle killing of 1788

By 1734, the border of the Cape Colony had been pushed over 400 km east of Cape Town to the Great Brak River. In 1746, Swellendam was founded 220 km from Cape Town. It was here where, in 1788, South Africa experienced its first – but sadly not its last – mass cattle killing.

The white farmers of the Cape firmly believed they were God's elect, destined to rule over the heathen natives, whom they were divinely entitled to dispossess and enslave. They were soon to discover that others, too, could invoke the Lord's name in their cause. In the late 1780s, a charismatic KhoiSan prophet from Swellendam named Jan Parel proclaimed to his brethren and sistren that the end of the world, and their torment, was nigh. D-day was set for 25 October 1788 – but only if the KhoiSan people slaughtered their white cattle; burnt their European clothes; built special new dwellings; destroyed the whites' farms, slaughtering the inhabitants; and attacked the Swellendam drostdy, the official residence of the landdrost (sheriff).

Parel told people he was immortal, and his apocalyptic prophecies struck a chord. The white farmers dismissed Parel as a joke. Some KhoiSan were sceptical but, as the fateful date drew closer, a growing number of others – particularly women – heeded his call. Slaves started deserting farms. Many white cattle were slaughtered.

Finally the settlers started to re-evaluate the threat Parel posed to them. The authorities marshalled troops, who quashed the planned 25 October assault on the drostdy and arrested many of Parel's followers. Parel disappeared into hiding but was later found and sentenced to hard labour. That Parel escaped the death penalty testifies to the settlers' nervousness that killing him might trigger another, perhaps more dangerous, insurrection. The KhoiSan, meanwhile, were left with their dreams of freedom trampled and their white cattle dead. The world did not end.

Millenarianism, the Battle of Grahamstown and cattle prophecies

By 1806, British troops had wrested control of the Cape Colony from the Dutch, and the VOC had been liquidated. British soldiers had flooded into the Cape, Grahamstown had been set up as a new military headquarters, and the amaXhosa restricted to the land east of the Fish River. The combination of increasing British militarism and spreading religious millenarianism – the belief that all wrong things will be cosmically righted at the appointed hour, following a cataclysmic event – created fertile soil for another cattle-killing movement, this time led by a man known as Makhanda, who also went by the name Nxele, and after whom Grahamstown was officially renamed in 2018.

Makhanda was a Xhosa prophet who had converted to Christianity. He took the religion – in an ecstatic form, imbued with an indigenous message – back with him when he returned to Xhosa territory to start preaching there. He claimed extraordinary powers for himself, such as the ability to be unharmed by weapons – hardly surprising, since he also claimed to be a son of God.

When Makhanda became an advisor to the paramount chief, Ndlambe, his message became yet more millenarian. In 'Not a Nongqawuse Story', her fascinating contribution to *Women in South African History*, historian Helen Bradford writes: 'He popularised the Flood. His Father would return, he prophesied, incinerating sinners with heaven's fire.' When the British supported Ngqika, an opponent of Ndlambe, as chief, the two Xhosa parties went to war. Ndlambe's troops vanquished their opponents. After this, Makhanda led a great battalion of 14 000 Xhosa – men, women and children – against the British in Grahamstown in 1819, believing that they would prevail against any weapons. This time, they lost – the biggest loss of life in any single frontier battle.

Makhanda fled to Gompo Rocks, on the coast near East London, where he threatened to throw himself into the sea. He also prophesied that the dead Xhosa warriors would return victorious and the abelungu would be driven into the sea – but only if the Xhosa killed all dun (grey-brown) and pregnant cattle. Many believed, and cattle were driven to the place of the prophecy and slaughtered. Ultimately, Makhanda did not leap into the Indian Ocean. Instead, he gave himself up to the British two weeks later. Makhanda was jailed on Robben Island and eventually died, apparently during a botched escape attempt, in 1820.

Even though Makhanda's prophecy never came true, it resonated with many amaXhosa and continued to spread through his son – particularly amongst amaXhosa living east of the Kei River – in subsequent waves of apocalyptic visions. Mphuthumi Ntabeni, the author of *Broken River Tent*, identifies this millenarian, religious sensibility as one of the reasons the prophecies of Mlanjeni, and later Nongqawuse (whom we meet below) were so readily accepted. (Ntabeni also points out that at this time, as later during the time of

Nongqawuse, there were many who did not participate in the cattle-killing movements.)

Prologue to war: the mass cattle killing of 1850

Nearly three decades after Makhanda's prophecy, another mass cattle killing took place, this time in British Kaffraria, an area in what is now the Eastern Cape.

The killing was a direct result of the actions of Sir Harry Smith, who was appointed governor of the Cape in 1847 and wasted no time putting in place laws aimed at forcing the Xhosa nation to transfer their affections away from cattle to sheep, since wool exports to Europe were fast becoming an important source of revenue. Native Commissioners were instructed to forbid chiefs from exacting fines in cattle. In cases of civil dispute concerning cattle, the offending animals were to be shot. Outrageously, Smith also forbade the payment of lobola in cattle, and – for good measure – outlawed the detection, or the employment of outside expertise to detect, malevolent magic or witchcraft.

In October 1850, Smith summoned all Xhosa kings and chiefs to a meeting in British Kaffraria. When one king, Sandile, failed to arrive, Smith summarily replaced him with a young white official, Charles Brownlee. Scandalised, Sandile sought counsel from Mlanjeni, a prophet. Mlanjeni – who was under the influence of Makhanda's son – advised Sandile to instruct those followers who were prepared to fight for him to slaughter one light brown or yellow cow. As long as these animals still walked the earth, Mlanjeni said, 'the nation will die'. He claimed slaughtering them would improve ancestral protection and make warriors who used a medicine he prepared immune to soldiers' bullets.

The slaughter of cattle quickly gathered pace, frightening white farmers, many of whom fled their farms. Smith dispatched 650 British troops to the Amathole mountains, where Xhosa warriors ambushed them, killing 12 soldiers. This started the eighth and penultimate frontier war between the colonists and the Xhosa, described by one historian as 'the longest, hardest and ugliest war ever fought in over one hundred years of bloodshed on the Cape Colony's eastern frontier'.

Particularly in its final stages, this was a war of attrition in which frustrated British troops burnt Xhosa crops and slaughtered or stole their cattle, causing widespread starvation. The conflict ended with an uneasy peace agreement between the Xhosa and a new governor, Sir George Cathcart, in March 1853. Mlanjeni died five months later, still uncaptured, of tuberculosis.

Lung sickness and Russian saviours

A month after Mlanjeni's death, in September 1853, a ship from Holland arrived in Mossel Bay with a shipment of Friesland bulls. The bulls, it turned out, were infected with lung sickness, a disease that had already claimed the lives of hundreds of thousands of cattle in Europe. Lung sickness is a horrific disease that effectively strangles cattle from the inside, resulting in a slow, painful death and a skeletal carcass. It is also highly infectious, and quickly spread through herds belonging to white settlers and amaXhosa alike.

Many herds were all but wiped out. By 1856, Phatho, a Xhosa chief, had lost 2 400 of his 2 500 cattle, while Phatho's brother, Kobe, had lost 130 cattle from a herd of 150. Witnesses at the time described scenes of devastation. Compounding the apparent revolt of the natural world against humanity, a severe maize blight and unusually heavy rains also hit the colony, destroying crops or causing them to rot in the fields.

When news reached South Africa that the British governor, Sir Cathcart, had been killed by Russian troops in the Crimean War in November 1854, several Xhosa prophets foresaw that Russians would arrive in mystic fashion to liberate their nation, providing the Xhosa first purified themselves by slaughtering their remaining cattle. Many believed, but the Crimean War ended in February 1856 and the hoped-for Russians never came.

Nongqawuse's prophecy and yet more cattle killings

Two months later, in April 1856, an orphaned Xhosa girl named Nongqawuse returned from a walk to the Gxarha River with her young cousin, Nonkosi, to report that she had met two mysterious strangers who told her that the Xhosa warriors of the past would rise from the belly of the earth to take up arms against the British, provided all living cattle were first slaughtered.

Nongqawuse lived just east of the Great Kei River with her uncle Mhlakaza, who thought he recognised the description of his dead brother and was convinced of the girl's story. He spread the word far and wide. Details were embellished with every retelling. Nongqawuse, it was now said, foretold an abundant world where the blind could see, the old became young and there were large herds of new, disease-free cattle.

When news reached the Xhosa kings, they sent emissaries to investigate. The emissaries could not see or hear the spirits, who still spoke through Nongqawuse alone, but they nonetheless returned to their courts as believers. In July 1856, paramount King Sarhili went to stay at Mhlakaza's homestead. One of King Sarhili's advisors was, not uncoincidentally, the son of Makhanda, who by then had moved across the Great Kei and continued to spread the word of his father's vision.

By the time King Sarhili visited, the girl was saying that she had seen 'a great hole in the bush and looked in, and she had seen there numbers of people long since dead who were quite alive, and an incalculable number of new cattle'. By some accounts, the spirits spoke to King Sarhili too. He endorsed Nongqawuse's prophecy, encouraging many more to believe.

There were sceptics, of course, including chief Ngubo, Sarhili's first cousin, who demanded to talk to the Nongqawuse's spirits. When Nongqawuse told him he would die if he did, he beat her and denounced her as an impostor. Ngubo failed to convince the believers they were wrong. Soon, hundreds of cattle were slaughtered, with believers instructed not to eat the meat but to throw it away and leave it to rot. Some sold their cattle instead, the resulting glut pushing prices so low that soon cattle changed hands for less than the price of their hides.

Yet there was no sign of the prophecy coming true. Believers started asking when the dead would rise and the new cattle would come. Under pressure, Mhlakaza announced that 16 August 1856 would be the night. The date came and went. There were no new cattle and no new people.

Dismayed, Sarhili ordered a halt to the slaughter of cattle and went to see Mhlakaza. How could Nongqawuse's prophecy be fulfilled, Mhlakaza asked, when the Xhosa nation had only half-heartedly followed instructions? Many cattle still lived. Many other cattle had been sold rather than slaughtered, meaning that their blood and bile had not been saved for the ancestors.

Sarhili promptly banned cattle sales and went to see Mhlakaza again. This time, the king reportedly saw the 'new people', further convincing him that mass cattle slaughter was the only way forward.

The British administration was at first mystified and then enraged, convinced that the cattle killings were a subversive plot. Sir George Grey, who succeeded Cathcart as governor in 1854, wrote to Sarhili, saying he regarded the king as the guilty party and threatening to 'punish you as such'. Sarhili replied via a messenger that he and his people had been ordered to kill their cattle and not cultivate their fields, and would obey the order. More and more Xhosa farmers abandoned their fields to wait for the new people and cattle to appear.

At first the Xhosa believers were buoyant. But by November, with food running short, they became desperate. People demanded to know of Nongqawuse when her prophecies would come true. Eventually, she told Mhlakaza that the new people would not come until the chief of the area, a cattle-slaughter sceptic called Nxito, came home. When Nxito duly did so in late November, word soon spread that 11 December 1856 would be the night.

When 11 December came and went with no new cattle and no new people, Sarhili and an assembly of chiefs went to the Gxarha River to meet Mhlakaza and Nongqawuse. The gathering was set for 3 January 1857, but the pair did not turn up, instead leaving messengers to tell the chiefs that the spirits were angry at sceptics who had failed to slaughter all their cattle.

The assembly parted ways amid much bitterness and recrimination. Travelling back to his Great Place, Sarhili attempted suicide but was stopped by his counsellors. Haunted by the thought that it was the failure to kill all cattle that was holding the spirits back, rendering futile all the carnage that had been enacted thus far, Sarhili slaughtered the remainder of his herd in mid-January. Others followed suit, and the killings again intensified. A new ascension day was prophesied – 16 February 1857 – when, it was said, the sun would rise late and would be blood red. And yet, on the day, the sun rose on time and was stubbornly yellow.

Aghast, Sarhili sent a message to a British administrator:

> I have been deluded into the folly of destroying my cattle and ordering my people to do the same; and now I shall be left alone, as my people must scatter in search of food; thus I am no longer a chief.

Disappointed believers attacked those who had not slaughtered their cattle. They looked, unsuccessfully, to the British for protection. Instead, the British administration saw an opportunity to extend the colony, take more Xhosa land for white settlement, and force more Xhosa people into the cash economy as labourers. In the words of Grey:

> They [the Xhosa] must be widely dispersed over the Colony and ... thus brought under the charitable influence of individual employers ... trained to habits of industry and imbued with Christian principles.

To achieve this, the British administrators distributed emergency food rations only to amaXhosa seeking work in the colony. They also stiffened the punishment for theft, which had risen in step with worsening starvation. The main punishment was deportation from British Kaffraria to north of the river Kei.

An estimated 40 000 Xhosa people died as a result of the cattle killing, mostly from starvation. Including deportations, the colony's recorded Xhosa population was slashed from 105 000 to 37 000 in 1857, and just 26 000 by the end of 1858. The Xhosa kings were forced to surrender more than 243 000 hectares of land, mostly around East London, which was given over to white settlement. Many of the Xhosa who ended up working for the colony ended up in its towns and cities, and Cape Town acquired its first substantial black African population.

Why did so many of the Xhosa believe Nongqawuse's prophecy? Why did they kill their cattle and abandon their fields? Wasn't it obvious to them that they would starve? The official line of the British administration at the time was that the prophecy was a ruse dreamt up by the Xhosa kings to justify war against their colonial masters. For many white people, the answer has always been that the Xhosa believed Nongqawuse because they are irrational and superstitious, because they allow themselves to be deluded by mumbo jumbo. But that seems more an insult than an answer. In the judgement of Jeff Peires, the historian on whose work this account of the cattle killing is largely based, the rigorous symbolic cleansing of a cattle killing appeared logical to many of the Xhosa people following the ravages of lung disease – which the Xhosa would have associated with witchcraft. Peires argues that the cattle killing was most intense in areas where lung sickness had already hit the hardest. To the affected Xhosa, it would have been evident that the world was in urgent need of cleansing – and the slaughter of cattle fitted with a world view that has, for as long as anyone can remember, associated cattle and their sacrifice with ritual cleansing and ancestral communication.

Peires also argues that what was new about this cattle killing was the combination of a tradition-grounded call for cattle slaughter and the Christianity-infused prophecy of resurrection. The seductive

18

Judeo-Christian notion of a day of judgement when all wrongs shall be righted had taken root in people's imaginations, whether they were converts or not. Once embedded, the belief was nourished by the daily tragedies of the Xhosa nation's defeat: the loss of land; foreign soldiers burning homesteads and crops and stealing cattle; stupid, oppressive rules intended to destroy the culture; sick and dying cattle; and diseased crops.

The idea of a purifying mass cattle killing, too, had become embedded in Xhosa culture by the time of Nongqawuse's prophecies. Mphuthumi Ntabeni describes the cattle killing that followed her prophecies as 'a coming into fruition of seeds sowed by Nxele when he said the dead warriors will rise, send whites back to the sea, and bring with them healthy cows'. Slaughtering cattle en masse to cleanse the nation may be unique, but the apocalyptic world view that underpinned the prophecies made by Nongqawuse and Makhanda/Nxele was not. Forty years earlier in Europe, during the Napoleonic wars, for example, many in Russia had considered French commander Napoleon Bonaparte to be the beast of the apocalypse foretold in the Bible's book of Revelation. In Leo Tolstoy's *War and Peace*, Count Pierre Bezukhov is convinced that Napoleon is the anti-Christ, and that his threatened attack on Moscow would be The Last Battle, heralding the end of the world. Mercifully for Muscovites, Bonaparte's Russian campaign, and with it the belief that he was Satan incarnate, collapsed before Russian millenarians had had the chance to do much damage.

Tragically for the Xhosa nation, though, their millenarians were afforded all the rope they needed. Peires sees the cattle killing as resulting in the final collapse of Xhosa national, cultural and economic integrity:

The majority of Xhosa accepted that the catastrophe of Nongqawuse was irreversible, and they took their places in the schools of Alice and the docks of Port Elizabeth to work out a new destiny inside the belly of the colonial beast. Grey had succeeded beyond his wildest dreams of turning them into 'useful servants, consumers of our goods, contributors to our revenue', and it was as an oppressed class within Cape society that they took up the continuing struggle for liberation. Independent Xhosaland was dead; Nongqawuse and Sir George Grey had irrevocably transformed the Xhosa nation into South Africans.

Historian Helen Bradford adds a rare and welcome gendered analysis to Nongqawuse's story. In 'Not a Nongqawuse Story' Bradford argues that, by the early to mid-19th century, the British army had severely undermined Xhosa patriarchy, because defeat in battle had weakened the legitimacy of their male leaders and effectively feminised Xhosa men. This, Bradford says, made more compelling the vision of the return of invincible fighters from a bygone era to force the hated invaders back to the sea: 'When Nxele promised rebirth of patriarchs armed to the teeth, when Nongqawuse told of the arrival of the warriors of whom Nxele had spoken, wearing antelope karosses, all were invoking pre-1812 days' – days when men were men. This erosion of traditional Xhosa masculinities, Bradford says, had created a space for spiritual leaders – male and female – to step into the power vacuum throughout the first half of the 19th century. Suggesting the value of a gendered interpretation of oral traditions, too, Bradford asks readers to consider oral sources describing Nongqawuse as a young, pregnant girl alongside vivid depictions of Makhanda's virile masculinity. She posits that contemporary praise poems that portrayed Nongqawuse as pregnant during the time of her prophecies hint strongly that this was no ordinary pregnancy. In the conclusion to Bradford's study, she suggests these early Xhosa historians were 'singling out Nongqawuse not for her prophecies, which were commonplace, but for being impregnated by an other-worldly messiah'. This cosmically ordained pregnancy revealed her link to the long-dead Makhanda, a man often referred to by contemporary amaXhosa as 'the Black Christ' and was taken as further proof of the validity of her message of deliverance to a battered, disorientated people in their confrontation with what was then the most powerful military machine on earth.

Beware the rinderpest

In the late 1880s, 40 years after Nongqawuse's mass cattle killing, Italian troops imported cattle to Eritrea for their military campaign in Somalia. The cattle were infected with rinderpest, a highly contagious and usually fatal bovine disease that had been cutting a swathe through 18th-century Europe for several decades, fuelled by wars that resulted in livestock tramping back and forth across the continent.

The disease swiftly travelled south through Africa, propelled mainly by transport oxen, crossing the Zambezi River in March 1896 and the Limpopo River into South Africa not long after. Here is a grim description of the disease from the *Natal Witness* of 6 May 1896:

> Experience soon guides the eye and ear, and the broken winded cough and the discharge of tears from angry-looking eyes are at once noticed. As the disease runs on, the animal becomes dull and disinclined to rise from the ground ... most will be affected by a watery and foetid diarrhoea, often tinged with blood. The temperature is very high and the breathing laboured ... ropey saliva hangs round the mouth and nostrils ... as the temperature falls, the animal becomes semi-comatose and weaker; muscles quiver incessantly, moaning and gulping increase, and about six days after an attack commences the beast dies.

At the time, South Africa was divided into the Cape Colony and Natal, under British control, and the Transvaal and Orange Free State, under the control of independent Afrikaner governments. The rinderpest epidemic – or, more correctly, the epizootic – proved to be one of the greatest challenges these governments would face, resulting in the deaths of more than 2.5 million cattle.

African cattle herds were the worst hit. By 1897, white farmers were reckoned to have lost 40% of their cattle, while African farmers had lost a staggering 90%. As well as facilitating spiritual intercession with ancestors, cattle were at the core of the African economic system, providing milk, draught power, transport, meat, clothing, crop fertiliser, building materials and a store of wealth and dowries. Cattle ownership was one of the main reasons many African people had not, thus far, felt compelled to take up the poorly paid manual labour on offer on white-owned farms or on the mines. The loss brought on by the rinderpest broke the economic backs of Africans throughout what are now Botswana, Zimbabwe, South Africa, Lesotho and Eswatini (Swaziland).

Among African communities whose herds were dying before their eyes, a popular theory was that the disease had been deliberately introduced by white people to destroy them economically and force them into service. One white magistrate in the Transkei district of Willowvale wrote that 'a bitter feeling sprung up against the umlungu who, in order to reduce them [Africans] to poverty with the view to enslaving them to the western province farmers and depriving them of their country, had struck at the root of their life'.

Afrikaner farmers often agreed. According to the British resident commissioner in Basutoland, Sir Godfrey Lagden, writing in January 1897:

We have information that many of the Boers along our border believe and have impressed it upon the natives that Mr [Cecil] Rhodes introduced the rinderpest as a policy to Matabeleland, the Transvaal, the Orange Free-State and Basutoland.

At the same time, many white people dismissed African conspiracy theories about rinderpest with racist scorn. Lagden wrote:

How characteristic of the Kaffir to have outbursts of fury without any apparent reason. It is hard, after all our efforts, to be turned on in such a way; but the word gratitude is unknown to natives.

The discovery of the viral nature of the epizootic proved that rinderpest was not, in fact, a white conspiracy to destroy black people. But then, many of the previous theories about rinderpest popular in the white community were proven false too. One belief, widely held among white people at the time, was that the unhygienic state of African wagon riders was responsible for the spread of rinderpest. When such riders crossed from Basutoland into the Orange Free State, authorities humiliatingly ordered that they be dipped, along with their cattle, in carbolic soap and bleach. The fine for evading a dipping was £5 or three months in prison. Many offenders also received a lashing. Another theory popular in religious circles was that God was the author of the calamity, in Old Testament-style retribution for the wickedness of his creation on Africa's southern tip.

The British colonial authorities and two Boer republics employed two strategies to stop rinderpest: they slaughtered infected animals and used fencing to control the movement of cattle from infected areas. More than 7 800 tonnes of barbed wire and other fencing materials were imported to South Africa from Britain in 1896. The Cape government stretched more than 1 600 km of barbed wire along the Orange River in 1897, keeping rinderpest out of the colony for a few months. But in the end, the fences failed. At some point, every time, the epizootic would leap the fence and rinderpest would race on unchecked, leaving cattle devastation in its wake. And slaughtering the animals only made matters worse by motivating farmers of all races to conceal their infected animals from the authorities, further encouraging the spread of the epizootic.

The big breakthrough came in February 1897 with the discovery of a vaccine by German bacteriologist Robert Koch, who had been brought in by the Cape Colony government on the bill of diamond magnates De Beers to find a cure. Prior to his arrival, Koch had already discovered the tubercule bacillus that causes tuberculosis in 1882 and the cholera bacillus in 1884.

Impressively, Koch rose to the challenge. His successful vaccine was drawn from the bile of rinderpest-infected animals. By the end of 1898, more than two million southern African cattle had been vaccinated, effectively ending the epizootic. For a time, many African farmers refused to inoculate their cattle because they didn't trust the government vets, who had already slaughtered hundreds of their beasts and used the rest to test various unsuccessful vaccines – often with fatal results. As a result, the epizootic was prolonged in African communities.

The rinderpest epizootic had far-reaching consequences for black South Africans. In addition to directly decimating their livestock wealth, the heavy (yet useless) restrictions on the movement of cattle from infected areas, at a time when many Africans made a living from riding ox wagons, put thousands of black people out of work, rendering them penniless.

Though they were not responsible for causing rinderpest, white businesspeople and administrators were certainly not shy about taking advantage of its impacts, following the coldly opportunistic tradition of the British authorities after the 1856 cattle killing. Writing in mid-1896 from Gaborone in Bechuanaland, where he was prospecting for diamonds, famed British imperialist Frederick Lugard said rinderpest would 'compel the native to work on the railway which will now become a famine relief'. In the same year, a government official from Elliotdale in the Eastern Cape wrote that

> ... the ravages of rinderpest, although reducing the natives to poverty, have not been without beneficial results, and the native has now learned humility to those to whom he is subordinate, and also the lesson that by work only can he live.

The same bureaucrat opined that Africans would only be happy when they work, alleging that the relaxed lifestyle that their cattle had previously allowed them to live had rendered them both lazy and discontented.

The secretary-general of the London Missionary Society also

weighed in, writing approvingly in late 1896 that rinderpest would drive the reluctant Batswana into the labour market. In November of the same year, the Chamber of Mines cynically cut mine wages by 30% and lengthened working hours, reasoning that poverty would force Africans to seek waged labour, whatever the conditions. The Cape government, which had annexed Bechuanaland, forced Batswana who were resisting the slaughter of infected cattle to work as indentured labour on white-owned farms in the Transvaal.

And then there was the fencing. Fences that started life as veterinary cordons mutated seamlessly into demarcators of a new colonial land grab. The Commissioner for Native Affairs in Zululand wrote that 'the destruction of African cattle gave the colony [of Natal] a most favourable opportunity for delimiting African lands which had thus been vacated'.

Despite the fears of many colonial officials at the time, seething discontent among African communities about the authorities' handling of the rinderpest epizootic, while sporadically erupting into a scattering of brief revolts, never evolved into a sustained uprising. The revolution would have to wait.

Koch, for his part, won a Nobel Prize for his work on tuberculosis in 1905.

The legacy of East Coast Fever

In 1904, just six short years after the end of the rinderpest epizootic, another deadly cattle disease hit South Africa. *Theileriosis*, or East Coast Fever, is carried by ticks and is still found in many African countries today.

The 1904 outbreak raged in South Africa for nine long years. The key to controlling East Coast Fever is to eradicate infected ticks, and one of the most effective ways of doing so is to dip cattle. By this time the Afrikaner armies of the Transvaal and Orange Free State had surrendered to the British. It was now the task of the victors to implement South Africa's first national compulsory cattle-dipping campaign.

The British authorities' implementation of the dipping campaign proved patchy and insufficient to contain the disease, but their taste for regulation – particularly regulation of black people and their livestock – on the satisfyingly scientific grounds of public health had been whet.

Seven years later, in 1911, one of the first pieces of legislation passed by the new Union of South Africa was the Stock Diseases Act. The Act made livestock dipping compulsory, required all cattle owners to report 'suspicious livestock deaths', introduced a plethora of controls on the movement of livestock, and made provision for the compulsory slaughter of diseased stock. Towards the end of the 1920s, the scope of the Act was extended to include the compulsory vaccination of cattle in African 'reserves'.

The Act was immensely unpopular among black farmers from the outset. People hated that it gave colonial authorities control over their livestock and, by extension, their lives. Many feared, correctly, that all this counting of animals would lead to new taxes. There were violent protests against the Act during its early years, particularly in the Mount Frere and Mount Fletcher areas of the Eastern Cape, where colonial authorities deployed troops to combat attacks on dipping tanks and sheds. Many of the Act's restrictions were lifted in 1930, but compulsory dipping remained, even in the bantustans, the so-called 'homelands' that the National Party formed after coming to power in 1948, where the Act remained in place and as reviled as ever.

The colonial authorities' appetite for regulating how African people should farm never left them. Not long after East Coast Fever died down, they imposed new controls on livestock numbers in African communities, this time in the name of tackling soil erosion. South Africa's cattle numbers had fallen during the early part of the 20th century because of East Coast Fever and the Second South African War, but after that the numbers grew rapidly, from under 4 million in 1904 to 8 million in 1920 and 12 million in 1939. Black people owned around half of the recorded national total until the 1930s, when the number shifted in favour of white commercial farmers.

In 1939, the government issued the Livestock Control and Improvement Proclamation, the country's first move to regulate livestock levels in communal areas. The proclamation demanded that livestock numbers be restricted to what government officials determined to be the land's 'carrying capacity', and allowed for 'extra' cattle to be either removed or slaughtered. Resistance was to be met with fines and imprisonment. The proclamation's implementation was suspended during World War II, but was reintroduced with vigour afterwards – and hated with passion by those to whom it applied.

In 1955, the apartheid government tasked a commission headed by Frederick Tomlinson to assess the economic viability of its planned bantustans. The Tomlinson Commission's main finding was that the bantustans were not economically viable, and required substantial investment, industrial development and more land. The Tomlinson Report also recommended that communal land tenure be stopped, communal land consolidated into commercial farms, and the newly landless evicted to cities to swell the urban proletariat.

Hendrik Verwoerd, then the Minister of Native Affairs, hated these recommendations, particularly the last one. He wanted the bantustans to absorb as many black people as possible; he certainly didn't want to export any more of them to 'white' South Africa. Verwoerd refused to implement the Tomlinson Report's recommendations, with one of the lasting impacts of that decision being that communal land tenure in the bantustans was left intact, as remains the case today.

Verwoerd was, however, enthusiastic about dipping and culling stock in the bantustans. He ordered that if the people there resisted, the punishment would be a reduction in income transfers to their governments from the apartheid state. The bantustan authorities responded by forcefully implementing stock culling during the early years, though by the early 1970s the situation had begun to relax.

In 1977, the Transkei government made a fresh attempt to

control livestock by introducing a livestock levy. The levy was hugely unpopular and met with massive resistance. It was eventually rescinded, to much popular acclaim, by General Bantu Holomisa in 1988, a year after he deposed then-Transkeian president Stella Sigcau in a coup d'état.

Cattle farming in democratic South Africa

Many white people in 1994 feared that the incoming socialist-leaning ANC-led government would increase state control over the economy. However, when it came to agriculture, the new government did precisely the opposite, swiftly relaxing many of the rules and regulations governing African livestock farming, including dipping requirements. The government also liberalised commercial agriculture, dissolving state agricultural marketing boards and ending the monopolies on livestock slaughter still held by council-run abattoirs.

The relaxation of state control has undoubtedly created business opportunities in the private sector, but it has also resulted in the dwindling of state veterinary vaccination services in communal farming areas. In addition to lower levels of vaccination, there is also not much livestock counting anymore. While this is perhaps a boon, seen from the perspective of the freedom of citizenry from state interference, it also makes the prospect of evidence-based agricultural policy-making from government less likely.

Another consequence is that ticks have reasserted themselves in communal areas, increasing the incidence of tick-borne cattle diseases. Ironically, many farmers in communal areas now demand that the government rebuild its capacity for livestock dipping and vaccination.

Centuries of colonial and capitalist assault have deprived contemporary African farmers of much of their economic self-sufficiency, forcing them to leave their farms and look for work elsewhere. Even so, the connection with cattle remains intact, with these gentle, large-eyed animals still looming large in these farmers' material and spiritual lives.

CHAPTER TWO

They bring us together: cattle in our homes and lives

The role cattle play in South Africa's contemporary African culture is a fascinating one. From subsistence farming families, who regard cattle as a source of material security and a critical link to the ancestral world, to urban politicians with multiple options to invest their wealth who nonetheless still choose to invest in cattle, they continue to retain their formidable presence in our collective mindset.

During the course of my research for this book, I travelled to northern KwaZulu-Natal to visit three subsistence farming families – the Mchunus, the Gumedes and the Ntombelas – to find out more about their cattle-rearing beliefs and practices. I also hopped north across the border, to Eswatini, where I met up with a cattle-farming local politician. Finally, I considered the case of our own president, who has even immortalised his love of cattle in book form.

The Mchunus

The day was wonderful and warm, the sky faintly smudged with thin wisps of cloud. Beneath the warmth lurked the kind of wintry nip that quickly becomes a chill when the sun goes down. It was a good day to meet farmers who live with their cattle.

With me were Lindiwe and Tom Ntombela, the nephew of the man who slaughtered the cow before my wedding. We were travelling along the N2 north of Durban, our destination, Zululand. The moment we turned off the highway, we found ourselves surrounded by communal farmland. Gone were the stoutly fenced, single-owner farms with their big houses, sheds, expensive equipment and shimmering crops of sugarcane or maize. Here, the cattle wandered hither and thither. There were few fences. The land was scrawnier and, scattered on the hills, were clusters of brightly coloured dwellings, each with a cattle kraal.

The journey took longer than expected and there was little daylight left when we arrived at the homestead of the Mchunu family. They had been waiting. We exchanged greetings, and two of the Mchunu wives silently disappeared, later to emerge clad in fine Zulu regalia. They were particularly proud of their isidwaba – beautiful, densely pleated, heavy leather skirts, the material for which came from the cattle slaughtered at their weddings. In this way, the cattle were assigned posthumously to protect and warm the women's intimate regions. Isidwaba may be worn only by married women, are difficult and time-consuming to make and are rarely seen these days – not least because they are expensive and weighty.

One of the wives also sported a spectacular isicholo, a traditional Zulu woman's hat that radiates in a widening circle from the crown of the head, decorated with intricate beadwork. Her hat was red and shaped to indicate that she was from the amaBomvu clan, whose women are also known for wearing red clay on their faces.

The women ushered us into a rondavel with half-brown, half-turquoise walls. Inside, several women and many children were already sitting. Lindiwe was instructed to sit with them, while Tom and I were seated opposite, where we were soon joined by ubaba Mchunu, the patriarch of the homestead. In the middle of the rondavel was a small, round ukhamba – a black pot – with a red bowl as a cap. It was filled with sweet-smelling maize beer.

We were soon drinking and chatting about farming life, and cattle farming in particular. When asked if he could imagine a life without cattle, Mchunu enthused:

No, it is not possible. Our cattle are a crucial asset. It is not just the milk and the ploughing they give us. It is the role they play in our spiritual life. When I see these cattle arriving at dusk, I am filled with excitement.

Cattle also play an important ceremonial role in the Mchunu household. Each of Mchunu's sons, he said, would need eleven head of cattle for each wife he took, with one to be slaughtered at the wedding:

We will pour the bile from this cow over the bride, so her ancestors will be connected to my son's house. And in the middle of this hut, where the ancestors dwell, will be a gourd with this bile that will hang until, one day, it perishes.

I looked up. Sure enough, numerous wizened remains of what I could now see were ancient cattle intestines hung from the thatch roof. The beer flowed as Mchunu warmed to his theme:

Our cattle bring our family together. Both when they are alive, and when we slaughter them. It brings harmony to us. Everyone has a role in the ceremonies, and when everyone comes to celebrate, it makes the occasion important and brings joy. When guests come whom we have not seen for a long time, it feeds our memories and creates new ones.

More people arrived, stooping to enter the hut's low entrance. Mchunu's second son, the two wives of his first son, and the sons of Mchunu's brother were among them. We were attracting quite an audience. The beer pot was passed round again.

Then the subject of slaughtering came up. In Zulu culture, only men are permitted to herd and slaughter cattle. When I asked why, some of the women suppressed giggles. Mchunu replied:

A woman cannot be allowed to use a knife to slaughter. ['It might give her ideas,' Lindiwe muttered to me in English.] A woman can use a knife to cut the meat, once it is cooked. And she is the one to dish up the meat, who will choose which parts of the animal will be served to which members of the family.

Serving food, it turns out, is a surprisingly complex matter, requiring deep knowledge of the culture. The job is usually handled by an experienced, senior wife. 'Men cannot be entrusted with such a task,' said the senior wife, shyly.

Compared to the prime cuts sold in supermarkets – which accounts for maybe 20% of a carcass – home-slaughtered beef is typically eaten from nose to tail, with different parts going to different people. The ubhedu (heart) is for the warrior in your life, and the ungungu or, more commonly, amaphuphu (lungs) for the coward. The umsila (tail) is for older men, and so is the ilulu (part of the small intestine), which usually goes to the owner of the slaughtered cow. The uluntu (the membrane covering a cow's gut) is for women, and so is the usu (large intestine). The men of the household are dished the intamo (neck) and inhloko (head); women get the isifuba (chest) and younger women the isikhaba (spinal area). Traditionally, the woman dishing up reserves a large portion of meat for the women who have been doing the hard work of cooking and serving and for unexpected, hungry guests who are sure to arrive.

The discussion turned to meat's taste and quality. Mchunu jumped in with some opinions about the difference between the meat of ceremonially slaughtered cattle and that of supermarket beef:

> There is no question. We love our slaughtered meat. It is soft to eat and it feels nourishing. The meat from supermarkets has been frozen, the blood is hard, and it has little taste. And when we slaughter we can use everything, not just what the butcher cuts for us.

When Mchunu became tired of talking, we went outside to see his cattle. Mchunu's face lit up when we arrived at the kraal, a short walk away:

> The feeling you get when your cattle return home, especially if they are fed and satisfied, is good. And when I look on them and count them, here in this kraal, that is a wonderful feeling.

Mchunu's herd was a mix of breeds, although their distinctive, beautiful hides indicated Nguni in the mix. Nguni cattle are often named after their markings and traits. Umkume is an outcast, shunned by the herd. Impusela is a calf whose mother has died and is itself slowly withering away. Ithekwa is a male calf that is still not sure what sex it is.

Mchunu's grandson, who was responsible for the herd, knew all their names. This one was itshe elimhlope, the white stone. And this one was umfaz' omnyama, a black woman. That one by the fence was u-anyanisi, onions. And the one just near it, that was uqoma ngesisu, the one who falls in love with her womb. Uqoma ngesisu, it seems, was particularly fertile. This younger one near her was mantombi, the little girl. 'See!' said the grandson. 'See how she is beautiful and how she flaunts that beauty.'

The cattle were indeed beautiful, but they were also worryingly thin. September is dry in these parts, and years of drought had taken their toll, leaving precious little grazing on the veld. A coal mine that had recently opened nearby also took copious volumes of water and was allegedly polluting much of the rest.

The herd consisted of about 30 cattle. A good number, Mchunu thought, though he reckoned he could do with more, saying: 'More is better, particularly if you have sons.' When I asked if he ever sold cattle, Mchunu said no. It had not yet come to that.

It was dark. The beer was finished and the younger children were yawning. The household would rise at dawn the next day. The mats were cleared away and a foam mattress and thick blankets brought for us. As we lay down to sleep, it was somehow reassuring that I could still just about make out those shrunken cattle intestines in the ceiling by the light of the flickering candle.

The Gumedes

The next morning we headed out along small roads to visit the Gumede family. After several hours, we turned in at a homestead of several rondavels in turquoise and brown. Two women appeared, having just returned from taking the cattle out to graze. Although they knew Tom, the women – who turned out to be Gumede's daughter-in-law and sister – did not want to talk about cattle. Only Gumede could comment, they said. Only after we promised to return for Gumede's thoughts did they relent.

The Mchunus had indicated that herding cattle was a man's task. Why, then, were Gumede's daughter-in-law and sister doing this work? MaNtengu, the daughter-in-law, explained:

> Things have changed. Before it was the boys who did this. But now they have to go to school and the men are working elsewhere, so it has fallen on our shoulders. The men do not like it, but they have no choice. On this one, they have had to swallow their pride.

I asked the women if they thought it worth their while to keep cattle, with all that effort and no men to share the load. They looked at me with pity. MaNtengu answered, gently:

> When a problem comes up in our household, cattle can be part of the solution. If our sons are to marry … we can use our cattle to pay lobola. Or if we slaughter and have a ceremony, there will be a hierarchical order to proceedings that helps our household.

She was referring, Lindiwe later explained, to the way ritual can ease the tensions that inevitably arise between wives in a polygamous household. Properly managed, a slaughtering ceremony can help cool the heat by reinforcing the social hierarchies between the living, and between the living and the dead.

Like the Mchunus, the Gumedes were passionately convinced that home-slaughtered meat tastes better than store-bought meat. 'Warmth and room temperature add flavour,' enthused MaNtengu, adding that ubende was made using the blood of a slaughtered beast, cooked with intestines. Meat 'with frozen blood' would just not work for such a delicacy.

The Gumede family was not as strict as the Mchunus about who could eat which cuts of meat. MaNtengu loved beef tongue and lung, although she admitted that in days gone by, the lungs were eaten only by young boys. Why the change?

Now everyone here eats whatever is provided on a plate. I think it is poverty that has changed all the old rules about who eats which parts.

The women had a day's work ahead of them, so we took our leave. But before we went, I asked one last question. 'In English,' I said, 'there is an expression, "stupid cow". Do you think cattle are stupid?' MaNtengu laughed out loud.

I don't know about your cattle, but our cattle are anything but stupid. We have told you what they do for us. How stupid is that?

When we returned later that day, Gumede was there. Gumede grew up among cattle within what is now Hluhluwe-iMfolozi Park. His father owned a herd of more than a hundred head, but was forcibly removed when the park was created, finally ending up a few kilometres away, in the exact spot where we were talking to Gumede.

Gumede explained that this was just one of his homesteads. He had three – one for each wife, although two had passed away – and each household had cattle. In total, he had about 40 cattle. 'There used to be many more, but we are suffering from drought, and they are dying,' he said wistfully.

Gumede said his sister and MaNtengu were doing a good job of looking after his cattle. He had followed protocol when assigning them this task, so it was unlikely that the cattle were dying as a sign of the ancestors' displeasure:

We had a ceremony. We did not slaughter, but we informed the ancestors that the women would be looking after the cattle because there was no one else to do the job.

Prepared as he was out of necessity to allow women to tend his cattle, Gumede would not countenance women slaughtering them:

> Woah, woah … wait now! There are some rules one cannot change. No. When it comes to slaughtering, anything can go wrong. One cannot take chances there. No. If these women notice something is wrong with a cow in my absence, they must contact me to ask what to do. And if the cow must be slaughtered, they must ask a man to do so.

Commercial farmers, and particularly white commercial farmers, tend to regard such beliefs as archaic, and getting in the way of the business of cattle farming, where the aim is to keep buying and selling cattle strategically for profit. All this cultural stuff, goes the scoff, is what keeps old-school African farmers like the Gumedes poor. I outlined this line of argument to Gumede. He thought for a while before calmly replying:

> White farmers are entitled to their point of view. They do not understand that our cattle, our living cattle, are part of our homestead. We understand there is money in cattle, but this is not our priority. Our priority is not to sell our cattle. We prefer to live from what we grow in our gardens and the milk from our cows, and only slaughter when the occasion is right. Sometimes, we will sell a cow if there is an urgent need of money – but only with great pain.
>
> Cattle are part of our lives. When we die, our bodies are wrapped in a cow's hide. And when we live, we wear their hides, their skins, connecting us to our cattle and to our ancestors. That is how it was, at least. Everything we had came from the world around us.

Gumede then asked a young boy to bring his Zulu regalia. When the boy returned, Gumede unhurriedly took off his trousers and shirt and pulled on the items, cheerfully identifying every item of clothing by name and which part of the cow it comes from. After a pause, he continued:

> We have compromised enough with you whites. We have really tried. We put on shirts and trousers and lost this connection with our cattle. But this love we have of cattle, we cannot compromise on that. It goes beyond the skins we wear, or the meat we eat. Perhaps it will be hard for you to understand, but we are asking that you accept it, this interdependence of ours with cattle.

We walked over to a nearby kraal, fenced with sticks and twigs. Gumede lovingly described each of his cattle. His face clouded over when the conversation turned to the subject of the nearby coal mine:

> Yes, it has given us some jobs. One of my sons works there. But we have had to uproot the bones of our ancestors to make way for it, and now we find that the mine is so thirsty – it is drinking up all our water. In fact, we are being treated like cattle …

Gumede warmed to his theme, lamenting that first his community had lost its grazing lands to the national park, and now their water was being taken.

> I have become poor. I am almost too poor to eat meat. Our cattle are so weak they hardly produce milk. We used to make amasi from their milk but now there is so little milk that we buy it from the shop. Life is not the same.

Gumede is right, I thought afterwards, life is not the same. Yet at the same time not everything has been lost, and it was reassuring to see that the old culture of living with cattle, as opposed simply to living off them, still thrives. Furthermore, as I explain later in this book, the way households like Gumede's keep livestock is far more environmentally sustainable than most commercial livestock farming, and as a result seems better placed to survive the growing call from environmental lobbyists to cull livestock as a way to preserve the planet.

The Ntombelas

The next day, Tom took us to his own family, the Ntombelas. Tom's uncle, the head of the household, was away, working in Johannesburg. A few days earlier, Tom had called him for permission to speak to his wives. The uncle agreed, although during our time there, he frequently called his wives on their cell phones to find out what was being said.

We spoke with the wives in a rondavel, the cement floor immaculately polished. What had happened, Lindiwe wondered, to the hardened cattle-dung floors of yore? Ntombela's eldest wife, Simphiwe, sighed:

> This was a job that used to be done by the young people. But it is hard work and must be done regularly. The children today no longer want to do it.

Ntombela had not been pleased to discover that the dung floor had been replaced by cement, worrying that their ancestors might not approve of the change. But nothing untoward had happened to the family so far, and his wives reckoned the ancestors understood that times had changed. Anyway, they said, the most important thing was that the household had not stopped performing ceremonies:

> The ancestors know that we still love and revere them.

It soon came out that Ntombela's herd was also in trouble. Twelve cattle had recently died, possibly of hunger but equally possibly, Ntombela and his wives believed, because something was wrong with the water. Fortunately, this loss had been balanced by the arrival of eight new cattle, courtesy of a lobola payment for Ntombela's eldest daughter. Ntombela was delighted, his wives said, and took the cattle out to pasture himself on his rare trips down from the city.

When I asked her about it, Simphiwe had an interesting alternative take on the English expression, 'stupid cow':

> It is true that cattle can be stubborn. You want them to go one

way, and then they go in the opposite direction, even if there is danger there. In this, they are just like people. So yes, in that sense, people can be stupid like cattle.

Ntombela's second wife, Phumzile, agreed – but with a caveat:

> The difference is that stubbornness is part of a cow's nature. But as people, we should listen to others' opinions.

Did they ever worry that they might be living in the past? Had money not replaced cattle as the true marker of wealth? The eldest wife replied.

> We hear young people saying that. But when trouble comes, will the bank help them? If there is a ceremonial function, they will need a cow, not cash. If they need cash, they can always sell a cow.

Phumzile added:

> Cattle make a home complete. The connection runs so deep that when a cow falls sick, it is often a sign that someone in the family will also fall sick.

That struck a chord with Tom, who recounted the story of another uncle, who died the day after one of his bulls keeled over without showing signs of sickness. Another bull died the day after the uncle's funeral. After we had all digested this information, Simphiwe continued:

> Cattle show that the family is solid, and they play a spiritual role too. Money sleeps in the bank, without any connection to the family … There is a challenge, though, that to have cattle, you must have someone to look after them when you are at school or at work. That has led some to prefer money and banks to cattle.

Like the Gumedes and Mchunus, the Ntombelas had no doubt that freshly slaughtered beef beat supermarket meat any time. According to Simphiwe, the difference was in the blood:

> When it is fresh, there is taste in the meat. But when the blood is cold, there is none.

Phumzile nodded her head vigorously, adding that the meat from supermarkets is just 'snow meat'. If it was just 'snow meat', why did they eat it?

It is our love of meat. When there is no meat on our plate, it means that we have fallen into deep poverty. We grow vegetables, and we love them. But our love of meat goes deep.

The Swazis and their cattle

Africa's love of cattle transcends borders and financial standing, as a trip across the border to Eswatini (Swaziland) soon led me to discover.

There is good grazing to be had in Eswatini, but in a country this size, inevitably, there is not much of it. About 75% of the country's people are subsistence farmers, grazing their cattle on Swazi Nation Land, which falls under the control of traditional leadership, much like communal land in South Africa. About 37% of Swazi land is privately owned, with vast sugarcane estates dominating the landscape.

After arriving in Mbabane, Eswatini's capital, I met with Ronnie Nxumalo, a senior veterinary officer in the government's department of veterinary and livestock services. Once pleasantries had been exchanged, Nxumalo got right to the point. Swazis like their cattle. Or, more accurately:

They love their cattle. Even if you put Swazis in storeyed buildings, in the modern way, I would like to believe they would still keep cattle. We are trying to promote commercialisation on the communal production system, but it is a real struggle, I can tell you. People do sell their cattle ... but not at the level we would like.

Nxumalo is right about modern Swazis still wanting to keep cattle, if the late David 'Lion' Shongwe is a good example to go by. A member of parliament for Mayiwane in Swaziland's northern Hhohho district before he died, Shongwe – a dignified, portly and modestly dressed man with a wry sense of humour – was part of the small percentage of Swazis who did not need to rely on the land for his livelihood. An accountant by profession, Shongwe had worked at Swaziland's Mhlume Sugar Mill for over 30 years before being elected to parliament. And yet, despite his relative wealth, Shongwe owned a feedlot with 25 cattle and had another 58-strong herd out grazing in Buhleni.

An MP's duties were onerous, Shongwe said when I met up with him, but he still found time for his cattle:

I go looking around the country for cattle whenever I get a chance. If I see a good animal, I try to buy it.

Because he didn't own a farm, Shongwe kept his cattle at Buhleni:

It is Nation Land. But I cannot afford my own farm. Perhaps you can help me? Every morning, I have to go and look at my cattle. Every morning. It is not too far. Parliament only starts at 2.30 pm so I usually have enough time. Although sometimes I have other tasks. When you are an MP everyone comes to you. For money and for everything. You end up being very frustrated.

Shongwe went to great lengths to explain that he did not keep cattle for traditional reasons, like his father did, or, he maintained, as most Swazis do:

No. This is for business. That is why I sell as well as buy. Most Swazis cannot bring themselves to do that. But in three weeks, I shall sell ten cattle. I am trying my best with my feedlot. I fatten up the cattle for three months and then I sell them to Swazi Meat Wholesalers. The problem is that I am finding that the maize, the grain is too expensive. It is hard for me to make a profit. I might give it up.

The cattle-loving president

Shortly before he ascended to the presidencies of the ANC and South Africa, Cyril Ramaphosa penned a book on cattle, *Cattle of the Ages*. The book consists mostly of beautiful, glossy photographs showcasing his highly photogenic herd of long-horned Ankole cattle, which, the book explains, Ramaphosa first obtained from Ugandan president Yoweri Museveni. Enamoured of the beasts, Ramaphosa went on to import Ankole embryos to South Africa for implant into local cows. He has since steadily built up his numbers to achieve what he says is the largest commercial Ankole herd in the country.

In the book, Ramaphosa confesses that he had no physical connection with cattle during his childhood. This contrasts the president's childhood to those of presidents Jacob Zuma and Nelson Mandela (though not Thabo Mbeki), both of whom herded cattle as young boys. Ramaphosa's father had herded cattle in Venda but abandoned them when he left to live in Johannesburg. This has given Ramaphosa some family memories of cattle and their place in human lives to draw on, though his own connection with cattle only began with his own post-1994 purchase of commercial farms.

Ramaphosa acknowledges in the book that South Africa has a land question to resolve, but he doesn't say much more than that. The main political point he ventures is that black people should be better enabled to become successful commercial farmers. He writes:

> The constraints imposed on many South African black farmers through the lack of grazing land have placed limits on their effective participation in profitable cattle breeding. These limitations will only be fully overcome when the country's land question is effectively resolved.

A little later, Ramaphosa writes that 'cattle can empower communities just as they did in the past', seemingly implying a more collectivist approach. But perhaps not. Like many of the things Ramaphosa says, these words can be taken in different ways and for the moment at least, it remains unclear whether the president knows what he wants on the land question, or whether he is as undecided as his party about how land reform and the future of rural South Africa should evolve.

Why we love them: an anthropological-environmental view

The role of cattle in 'traditional' African societies has fascinated outsiders for a hundred years. In 1926, American anthropologist Melville J Herskovits wrote about the 'cattle complex' that governs the lives and social organisation of people across much of East Africa, particularly through dowries and tributes. The term 'cattle complex' subsequently became popular among white settlers in East Africa, who believed it accurately captured what they regarded as African people's unhealthy obsession with cattle.

In the 1970s, a new generation of academics countered this view, arguing that the African attachment to cattle was a logical response to circumstance, since cattle were both a store of wealth and an insurance against calamity.

More recently, the late historian Jeff Guy argued that, at least when it came to the Zulu people, even this apparently more enlightened perspective is misconceived, since it rests on the fallacious assumption of 'the universality of the accumulation of goods as capital'. While pre-colonial Zulu society clearly valued the products derived from cattle – the milk, meat, and leather – the cattle's true worth lay not in their financial but in their social value, linked to their role in the cycle of production. The labour power of women, both as workers and as bearers of children, was another part of the same cycle, requiring cattle in the form of lobola payments. Men's wealth in pre-colonial times, Guy argued, therefore lay not in accumulating cattle or wives, but rather in accumulating via them 'the production of animate life'.

Pre-colonial Zulu homesteads were economically self-sufficient. It was this independence that the colonial authorities set out to destroy through military conquest, land occupation, the burning of houses, the theft of cattle, the destruction of grain and the dispersal of people. Once the conquest was nearly complete, the colonial administration further undermined this self-sufficiency of African households by imposing a 'hut tax'. The hut tax forced households to send family members in search of paid work, in order to generate the necessary income to pay the tax.

The arrival in South Africa of industrial mining in the late 19th century created huge demand for labour. The colonial authorities in what was then Natal calculated that this demand could best be met not by further annihilating Zulu homesteads, but instead by preserving them, albeit in a significantly modified form. The two homestead features the authorities wished to be retained were female agricultural and domestic labour, and patriarchal rule by male kraal heads. To be dispensed with, however, was the kraal heads' legal control over land. The 1891 Code of Native Law classified all 'natives' as either kraal heads or their dependants and bestowed on the former legal responsibility for the latter, including their earnings and debts. Kraals were then grouped under district headmen who were under the authority of the tribal chief, who in turn owed loyalty to the British crown.

Yet without a guarantee of land, plus the continued imposition of hut taxes by the state, the economic self-sufficiency of homesteads further eroded despite the authorities' professed intentions, with more and more of their members steadily sucked away into faraway cities and the wage economy. Guy's depressing conclusion was that while the idea of home has remained strong in Zulu homesteads to this day, the social and economic forces that once gave that meaning have been sapped by over a century of capitalism, colonialism and apartheid, leaving homesteads economically marginalised, and the productive energies of their members diverted instead 'into the service of an intrusive new order'.

The three Zulu homesteads I visited have, it is true, long been robbed of their economic self-sufficiency. They have few resources to compete in a capitalist economy and the productive energies of their members have largely been diverted to city jobs or to labouring in the coal mine right on their doorstep – the same mine that could be indirectly killing the few scrawny cattle on which they depend for their physical survival and spiritual health.

Meanwhile Ramaphosa, the country's president, despite a largely cow-free youth, today feels so strongly compelled to engage with cattle that he is breeding Ankole, a breed new to South Africa, and has published a book about them. Ramaphosa's love of cattle seems to mirror that of the rural households, but as a farmer, the president's approach appears to be the same as that of white commercial farmers.

And yet, economically sidelined though the rural households are, the way they keep their cattle – in small numbers, on marginal land ill-suited to crops and without the use of many purchased inputs – and the way such households eat them from snout to tail is more environmentally sustainable than standard commercial livestock farming. I believe the way these households keep their herds should be a guiding light for how to sustainably farm and consume beef in South Africa, at a time when both climate crisis and nutritional concerns are posing increasingly serious challenges to commercial farming methods.

CHAPTER THREE

Tucking in: the culture of eating beef

At 18.5 kg per person, South Africa's annual average beef consumption is the highest in Africa and is, by anyone's reckoning, a fair amount of meat. That figure is, however, slightly lower than the United Kingdom's annual average of 19.8 kg, and is way, way less than the 60 kg guzzled annually by the average Uruguayan, who leads the world in this regard.

South African beef consumption per head continues to rise, but slowly. Although price plays a part in this, the key underlying reason appears to be rapid urbanisation, which pushes up rates of chicken consumption all over the globe. Eco-maverick author Simon Fairlie explained the process in the following way:

> As human civilisation urbanises ... so our livestock becomes urbanised ... The pastoral steer and rural cow yield to the agrarian and proto-urban pig, which in turn is now yielding to the megapolitan broiler hen.

Despite the rise of chicken, the nation's love of beef is holding firm. We are constantly dreaming up innovative recipes and reasons to eat beef in its various, uniquely South African forms. Vegetarianism and veganism are fast on the rise, increasingly driven by concerns about climate breakdown, but for the time being, whether it comes as biltong or boerewors, a steakhouse or a shisanyama, beef remains a common thread that continues to bind South Africans together.

This is how we eat: biltong

Biltong needs no introduction to South Africans. More or less everyone is intimately familiar with these dried strips of meat – usually beef, but often game – so much so, in fact, that many babies literally cut their teeth on it.

The San were the first people on this land to hang and dry meat and had already been doing so for thousands of years when white settlers first arrived and copied them. Contemporary accounts describe trekkers tenderising meat from the game they had shot by placing it under their saddles as they rode. Soon, people were adding vinegar, salt, sugar, coriander and other spices to the meat as it dried.

Recipes for biltong began cropping up in Cape newspapers in the second half of the 19th century, with the first biltong recipe in a locally produced cook book appearing in Ms AG Hewitt's *Cape Cookery*, published in 1889. In his 1946 book, *Leipoldt's Cape Cookery*, the celebrated Afrikaans poet and botanist C Louis Leipoldt offered the following recipe:

> Trim into an even, elongated oval. Make a mixture of salt, pepper, saltpetre, crushed coriander and fennel seed and moisten it with vinegar; rub this into the meat, and cover the meat with it for a few days, rubbing the mixture every day. Hang the biltong in a draught and continue the rubbing with the spicy mixture till the outside is wind-dry. Tie a cheese cloth round it and hang it in a chimney for a couple of weeks to get thoroughly smoked.

Leipoldt insisted that biltong should be cut into 'exceedingly thin slices and eaten on bread and butter', and that it should be 'moist with a modicum of fat'. Cut thicker, he said, beef biltong should be fried like a bacon rasher or grilled and served with fried eggs.

These days, biltong is made using much the same ingredients, although sugar and Worcestershire sauce are sometimes added. (Leipoldt would have been sure to disapprove.) I have not come across anyone smoking biltong, though, and many insist that biltong is 'never' smoked.

Gram for gram, biltong is probably the most expensive beef there is – far pricier than rump or fillet steak. Being as delicious as it is, the wealthy tend to gobble their biltong quickly. Those with less cash but more discipline, however, can chew on it for hours, and when eaten this way, biltong becomes among the best value meat there is.

This is how we eat: boerewors

The poet Antjie Krog has written evocatively about boerewors as the physical manifestation of a well-run farm, with the patriarch and his men raising and providing good-quality meat and the matriarch, armed with a prized, secret family recipe, organising her kitchen staff into the production line required to make the perfect wors.

Industrially produced supermarket boerewors is a far cry from such a farmer's kitchen, even though this is still how people often like to think about this coiled sausage. Tapping into this narrative, one large retailer holds an annual competition to find the nation's best boerewors recipe and then commits to using this recipe in all its stores. Demonstrating the country's appetite for boerewors, the same retailer says it sells more than 8 000 km of the sausage – five times the distance from Cape Town to Johannesburg – each year.

This is how we eat: processed meat vs offcuts

With meat becoming steadily more expensive relative to income in recent years, many South African households have chosen to trade down on the quality of the meat they eat, moving away from fresh cuts in favour of processed meats like polonies and viennas, in order to maintain their preferred meat consumption volume.

The problem with compromising on the quality of beef that one eats, however, is as much about nutrition as it is about taste. Processed meats like polonies and viennas are manufactured using what the meat industry optimistically calls 'lean finely textured beef' (LFTB), which consists principally of trimmings – those parts of cattle that cannot otherwise be sold, including connective tissue, cartilage and sinew. To make LFTB, the trimmings are heated, the melted fat is removed, and the remaining meat briefly frozen and squeezed through tubes sprayed with ammonia or citric acid to kill *E. coli* and *Salmonella* bacteria. Unfortunately, these additives make it difficult for many micronutrients to survive. Certainly, it is otherwise hard to understand why there are several recent patent applications in the United States for processes intended to minimise this loss. One such application, dated 2013, describes 'combining a mixture of fat particles … and lean particles … with a saturated aqueous fluid … causing the fat particles to rise in the fluid and collecting the lean particles. The saturated fluid *reduces the depletion of micronutrients from the lean*' (my emphasis).

Even though LFTB still contains nutritional heavy hitters like iron and zinc, the LFTB process changes its nutritional profile in a way that frying or stewing beef simply does not. To make matters worse, LFTB is typically produced from the meat of feedlot-fed cattle, which itself is less nutrient-dense than that of grass-fed cattle.

In mitigation, LFTB manufacturers argue, polony, viennas and the like use unpalatable yet serviceable offcuts from cattle that would otherwise be wastefully discarded. In a food-insecure country like South Africa, where studies have found that as many as a third of children are malnourished, they maintain it would be a crime to waste any food. As it is, and scandalously, according to the World Wildlife Fund a third of the total food produced in this country – 10 million tonnes – goes to waste every year. The Centre for Scientific and Industrial Research (CSIR) estimates the value of the food wasted annually at R61.5 billion.

The argument seems compelling until you consider that there are many alternative uses for bones, cartilage and cheaper cuts that do not involve destroying flavour, adding ammonia and spinning the meat in centrifuges. This is gloriously demonstrated at the annual

Slow Meat festival, where competing South African chef schools are challenged to create innovative new dishes out of one prime cut and one offcut from an Nguni cow. The innovative, nutritious meals that have been created include bone marrow custard mixed into bread, liver parfait with beetroot dust, and pastry cones made with rendered fat filled with amasi and homemade ricotta. At the 2016 festival in Soweto, the chefs produced an impressive 400 portions of food from just one carcass, showing meat-eaters that it is possible to consume more of a cow than the 20% or so that constitutes its prime cuts and best stewing beef.

Even the Banting diet has taken to promoting more affordable cuts of beef. Banting is a popular diet that is commonly understood to recommend eating fewer carbs and more meat, although in truth it is more about increasing fat intake. The perceived focus on meat has exposed the diet to frequent accusation that Banting is a rich person's diet that does not speak to the country's real nutrition needs. Keen to combat this impression, in 2015 scientist Tim Noakes – a staunch promoter of the diet – and actress Euodia Samson started a Banting programme in Ocean View, an impoverished Coloured township near Cape Town. The programme concentrated on promoting cheaper cuts, including kidneys, brains and trotters.

The initial results were promising, at least according to media coverage. In December that year, Ocean View resident Priscilla Clayton was quoted in *The Mercury* as saying she was not only losing weight but that Banting was saving her R400 a month in groceries. According to Clayton, her grocery bill had gone down because eating high-fat food and fewer carbs was making her less hungry, so she snacked less, and thus bought fewer cakes and crisps.

An increased use of offcuts would make skinnier breeds of cattle like the Nguni (or Ramaphosa's beloved Ankole) more viable, not only for specialist breeders and lovers of their hides, but for regular beef consumers too. Sadly, this is not the way the market is going. The meat sellers I spoke to have noted a decrease in offcut and offal sales to the public. The traditional ways of eating or otherwise using every part of the cow, from horns to tail, are falling away in favour of chemical-sprayed processed alternatives that bear little or no resemblance to the meat from which they are derived.

This is how we eat: kosher beef

Jews were among the first European settlers in the Cape, even though a Dutch East India Company ban on non-Christians immigrating meant they had to keep their religion under wraps until 1820 – a full 170 years after European settlement began. In those early days, Jews in South Africa played little or no role in cattle farming, although some of the Lithuanian Jews who came to South Africa went on to become successful cattle traders in Zambia (then Northern Rhodesia).

Today, South Africa's Jewish community is concentrated in Johannesburg, where a little over 60 000 Jews are serviced by a dense network of kosher delis and restaurants. The oldest functioning kosher butchery and deli in the city is Nussbaums, which specialises in salted and cooked brisket, otherwise known as 'salt beef' and 'corned beef' – quintessential Jewish beefs the world over.

According to Ian Lurie, owner of Nussbaums, business is good. Although the number of Jews in the country has been in gradual decline since 1994 due to emigration, Lurie says the remaining number seem to be growing more observant. He speculates that this might be because Jewish families are choosing to send their children to Jewish rather than government-run schools.

Lurie is right. South African Jews are becoming more observant. Today, around 80% claim to be Orthodox, one of the highest rates for a Jewish community worldwide. There are still not enough practising Jews, however, to sustain a kosher abattoir. Instead, Nussbaums takes over at an abattoir in Krugersdorp on the West Rand for a day or two a week.

This is how we meet: the home braai

According to C Louis Leipoldt, the Afrikaans poet and culinary commentator on historical cuisine, the early white settlers to the Cape rarely braaied or even fried their beef, preferring to pot-roast, boil, pickle, or dry it.

Things have certainly moved on a long way since then, and for many, many years the braai has sizzled right at the heart of South African cuisine. Some people go even further, embracing the braai as *the* embodiment of South African heritage. For over a decade now, many people – apparently mostly drawn from white, more affluent sectors of the population – have celebrated 24 September, a public holiday officially designated as Heritage Day, as 'National Braai Day'. That this is the case is largely thanks to the efforts of one Jan Scannell, a thirty-something Afrikaner from Stellenbosch, who used to be a chartered accountant. Bored by his job, Scannell packed it in in 2005 and threw his energies into creating a long-standing dream of his – National Braai Day.

I met with Scannell one windy Cape Town day, when he told me that the concept, simply enough, was that everyone should braai on the same special day, have a merry old time, and feel good about being South African:

> I thought … why don't we South Africans get a day? Like the Americans have Thanksgiving and the Irish have Saint Patrick's? There's Australia Day, or Queen's Day in the Netherlands. I really like that one. Everyone dresses in orange.

Scannell selected Heritage Day, the day officially set aside for South Africans to 'celebrate their culture and the diversity of their beliefs and traditions'. Before 1994, 24 September had been Shaka Day, commemorated by the Zulu nation as the sad anniversary of their king's assassination in 1828 by his two half-brothers, Dingane and Mhlangana.

Twenty-plus years since democracy, popular awareness of the intended significance of Heritage Day remains decidedly patchy, with many people indeed seeing the holiday as an opportunity for a big, fat braai in the spring sunshine. Scannell tapped into this sentiment, unofficially changing his name to Jan Braai and cannily persuading Archbishop Desmond Tutu to become a patron early on, buttressing the initiative's rainbow nation credentials and protecting it, to a degree, from accusations that it is, at heart, a marketing ploy.

Scannell's main coup – and a key reason National Braai Day is as successful as it is – was winning over the supermarkets. Every year now, starting around mid-August, supermarkets enthusiastically promote all things braai. Step into any store during this period and, somewhere near the entrance, you will probably find a display of charcoal, firelighters, matches, tongs, booze, a South African flag or two, and lots of chops and wors.

After I met Scannell, I told Lindiwe about our chat. She wanted to know why Scannell, as an Afrikaner, had chosen a Zulu public holiday and not one linked to Afrikaner culture – like the Day of Reconciliation on 16 December. It seemed a fair question, so I rang up Scannell to ask him. His reply was characteristically frank:

I checked [Reconciliation Day] out with the retailers, and they wouldn't look at it. By that time they are fully busy with Father Christmas and jingle bells. They can't take time out from that to push the braai. And you obviously can't do it in winter either. But September is a quiet month for the supermarkets, so they welcomed the opportunity.

The resulting blend of marketing and nation-building patriotism is an uneasy one. Scannell has come under fire from the aggrieved National Heritage Council, which claims he hijacked Heritage Day and reduced the country's diverse heritage to a love of grilled meat. Scannell has also been accused of making South Africa's unity look too easy, for propagating the illusion that the bitterness of the past and the inequality of the present can be erased by chowing down on some chops. As blogger Herman Wasserman wrote on Africaisacountry.com:

> To say that this activity unites us is more or less the same as saying that just because we all drive on the N1 we are all going to the same address … Let's not allow the smoke to get in our eyes. Let's not forget that we're still a nation of people who can afford a chop-and-dop, and those who can't.

Responding to these criticisms, Scannell has come up with a new slogan that acknowledges government initiatives to persuade South Africans to celebrate their heritage: 'Unite around a fire: share our heritage and wave our flag'.

That might keep the Heritage Council at bay, but it does not erase Wasserman's point: that Braai Day is built around a fantasy – a sunlit advertising-industry version of unity that ignores the country's real divisions and challenges. In an apparent response to this, the design of the National Braai Day website (braai.com) draws heavily on Struggle-era imagery. At the time of writing, the banner topping the site featured an image of a black fist clenched in the air, holding a pair of braai tongs, with the payoff line, 'Join the revolution to unite 50 million people'. The Jan Braai Facebook page (Facebook.com/janbraai) echoes the theme, with a logo reading, 'Unite around a fire.'

Heavy-handed marketing techniques can only spin the realities of life so far. The tradition of inviting friends over to watch the game and throw a slab of beef on some coals is perhaps not as widespread as wealthier South Africans might think. Many less affluent urban households prefer to serve their guests a well-seasoned beef stew using cheaper cuts, bulked up by fresh vegetables and cooked until the meat is so tender it falls off the bone (which is most definitely in). It remains true, however, that braai culture has become firmly established in townships across the nation in the form of the shisanyama. Shisa means hot, usually referring to fire, and inyama means meat. Combined, the two words literally mean fired meat. In practice, the term refers to a restaurant, typically near a butchery, where patrons select their meat, the restaurant braais it and serves it with drinks to be eaten on the premises.

This is how we meet: the shisanyama and the steakhouse

Mzoli's Place in Gugulethu, Cape Town, is an internationally fêted traditional shisanyama with a butchery on the side. The restaurant part of it consists of a large terrace filled with plastic tables and chairs and covered with a tin roof. A few more seats are crammed into a small space outside. On weekends the place heaves, with hundreds of customers gorging themselves merrily on huge meat-and-pap platters. In one corner sits a headphoned DJ who plays a fine selection of kwaito and house music.

In the kitchen, several large wood fires blast an intense heat. Over the fires, tended by an army of cooks, are huge grills filled with steaks. The men work at speed, never once burning the meat. Perspiring waiters constantly rush in to place orders, returning soon to whisk the piled platters away.

Mzoli's founder, sixty-something, Presbyterian churchgoing, Mzoli Ngcawuzele, was born in Cape Town's central district but forced by the government to relocate with his family to a dusty patch of ground called Gugulethu, 15 km away, in 1963. Today, Gugulethu is a tightly packed township of over 100 000 people. But back then, Ngcawuzele recollected, Gugs was 'just bush'.

Ngcawuzele believes in Black Consciousness, coming to the philosophy as so many African people of his generation did, during the student uprising of June 1976:

The 1976 uprising was the turnaround. I learned that I am black and proud. That is me. I learned that you must know who you are.

For both pragmatic and ideological reasons, Ngcawuzele's Black Consciousness-inspired business vision did not exclude non-black people. Instead, he welcomed them:

> You must know how to put together the chemistry of a place so that everyone can feel comfortable. We have made a space where people from different cultures can come together, to enjoy themselves and to eat our meat. Our meat unites people and communities from all walks of life.

For Ngcawuzele, selling beef is about more than making money. It is also about uplifting Gugulethu. When visitors come to Cape Town, he wants to see Gugulethu and Mzoli's feature alongside Table Mountain, Robben Island and the Waterfront on their list of must-sees. Ngcawuzele has come some way towards achieving this goal. Mzoli's is internationally famous, receiving a four-star rating on TripAdvisor and routinely featuring in travel articles on Cape Town published by the likes of CNN, *The Telegraph* and Forbes.

Despite his success with the well-moneyed market, Ngcawuzele insists he will never forget his Gugulethu regulars. In addition to its various meat dishes, Mzoli's also dishes up inexpensive platefuls of umngqushu, otherwise known as samp and beans. The dish usually takes hours to prepare – hours that Gugulethu commuters do not usually have to spare.

It is perhaps fitting that Ngcawuzele started his career selling sheep and cattle intestines from the back of his truck. Although the meat wholesalers I spoke to have detected a shift away from tripe within African communities, it was still popular then and certainly liked enough to sustain Ngcawuzele's early endeavours and help him open a shisanyama in 2000.

Ngcawuzele doesn't care whether the beef he sells at Mzoli's is grass- or feedlot-fed (see Chapters Four and Eight for more on this) – and neither, he reckons, do his customers. What they want, he said, is large helpings of tender beef, which means category A, with not too much fat, but not too little, which means category 2. Once you have that, he said, all you need is a good fire, good cooks, strong spices, and, of course, a sauce with punch.

The steakhouse is the more affluent population's answer to the shisanyama – a place where you can go to have others serve you a meaty comfort meal, typically with chips or a jacket-baked potato. While some specialist steakhouses demand eye-watering prices, several restaurant chains make it their business to keep their prices lower to attract a more family-oriented clientele. Chief among these – quite literally, given its exhaustingly Native American styling – is Spur.

There seems to be a Spur in every South African town and city. In many of the smaller dorpies, it is the only sit-down restaurant there is. Spur's menu is classic steakhouse: beef steaks and burgers take pride of place, while chops and chicken play supporting roles. Salad keeps a low profile.

The first Spur was opened by Allen Ambor in Cape Town in 1967. The name referred, of course, to the spur on a cowboy's boot. (Thanks to American Western movies, cowboys and Indians were big all over the world in the 1950s and 1960s, and the theme of white settlers violently displacing indigenous people from their land resonated in South Africa.) The restaurant had a spur-themed logo and was only legally permitted to serve whites. In those days, Spur was much more cowboys than Indians.

Then, in 1986, there was a major shift. The cowboy-themed spur logo disappeared, replaced by an illustration of a noble-looking, strong-jawed Native American chief in full-feathered headgear, behind him a classic Western setting sun. The logo has changed a few times since, but the big chief and his feathered headgear have remained. Ambor explains his reasoning at the time:

Moving from cowboys to Indians wasn't a hard-headed business decision. It was how I felt. I was thinking in the 1980s about what was going on in South Africa. I wanted to create a signal to people of colour that they were welcome. That was why we changed the logo to a Red Indian. I mean ... Red Indians are a highly respected tribe with a spiritual, creative side. They also had a history of abuse against them, as it happened.

It was a canny move. Native Americans, though obviously non-white, were at the same time sufficiently non-South African for even apartheid-supporting white people to accept in a restaurant motif. Black South Africans, meanwhile, were being given a signal – albeit a very discreet, even covert one – that they could be 'Spur people' too.

Today, more than a generation since 1994, the cowboys survive only obliquely in the restaurant's name, and the Native Americans have completely taken over. The tablemats and seat covers are designed to look like cowhides. The lampshades have an ersatz Wild West feel. There are cartoon drawings of Native American youths with head feathers on the laminated menus, and children are invited to join the 'secret tribe'.

Yet while honey-coloured young cartoon squaws are everywhere in Spur restaurants, there is still no imagery of African people. The clientele these days is pretty mixed and, mostly, things work out although in early 2017 a furious confrontation in a Johannesburg Spur between a white man and a black woman over a playground fight between their children – was filmed and, inevitably, went viral. Spur staff were heavily criticised for doing too little to intervene. To atone, Spur banned the man from its restaurants. Numerous whites from the man's home in North West province launched a Spur boycott in protest, though by the end of the year customer numbers were said to be back up, suggesting that a love of keenly priced burgers and steaks had overcome the protesters' sense of racial grievance.

CHAPTER FOUR

You need to maximise: the economics of industrial beef

Beef constitutes roughly 60% of fresh meat sales by volume in South African supermarkets. Moving all that meat from farm to plate involves a supply chain that starts with breeders, ends with supermarkets or butchers, and includes auctioneers, feedlots and wholesalers along the way.

In contrast to the warm affection rural African farmers show their cattle, in the industrial beef complex these animals are a means to an end, whether for their uteri or for their meat. Each step in the supply chain is calibrated to extract maximum profit before the animal is shunted on to the next step of its doomed journey.

This chapter examines the ins and outs of the industrial beef complex, examining how things turn out in practice when beef production is guided by one core principle: more meat for less time and lower cost.

The breeder

Mike Wiechmann is a Simbra cattle farmer and stud farmer based in Otjihangwe, Namibia. I reached his farm one evening after a long, dusty drive, bumping past wandering cattle in the dusk before reaching the homestead. I had only been in the Wiechmann kitchen a short while when a shortwave radio startled me, crackling loudly into action. Through the static came a succession of voices speaking German. It was eight o'clock, time for the white farmers in the area to do their nightly security check-in. Tonight, Wiechmann translated, everyone was fine.

The farm had originally belonged to the parents of Wiechmann's wife, Erica, who started farming there in 1965. On taking over the property, Wiechmann changed things a little. Now, he said, he was in the high-tech stud business, importing embryos from the United States to transplant into local cows to carry to term:

> This is how it works. First, you inseminate the cow. Then the cow gets flushed. You average six to seven embryos per flush. Some cows give twenty. You make sure that you inseminate them with good semen, and once you've inseminated them, you flush the embryos a week or ten days later. Then later we separate the embryos out in the lab. At that point, you have to have your receiver cows ready. They should all be on heat … In total you might get twelve calves from each receiver cow. And on the embryo flushing side, you can get sixty embryos from just one cow.

Embryo flushing. This was new to me. I asked Wiechmann why he was using American cattle genetics. Would it not be better to use southern African genetics instead? Wiechmann conceded, saying he knew as a Namibian that African cattle genetics were better adapted to local conditions than were American ones. But, he said, in genetics you always need variety. He returned to his description of the flushing process:

> You inseminate the cows again a couple of months after you've flushed them. You can do it with a cow three times in a row. After that, you can't do it anymore, but she can still be used for ordinary calving.

All this embryo flushing, I ventured, sounded tough on the cows. Wiechmann shook his head.

No! That's what people think. But in fact, the cows don't feel anything. I assure you. The best we ever had from embryo flushing one cow was 60 calves in a single year. That was something!

Before I could ask why, if flushing was indeed so benign, you could only flush a cow three times before it all became too much for her, Wiechmann returned to the business side of the venture:

On this farm, we produce commercial oxen, stud and heifers. The critical thing in our business is that our calves survive. They have to. This is an expensive operation, seriously expensive. But to get the best genetics, you have to do this. The thing is this. It is hard to import cattle into South Africa, or anywhere. There are all kinds of restrictions, and that is right, there need to be. But, you see, it is easy to import embryos. The embryos are all frozen in liquid nitrogen. They are very easy to transport.

Transporting embryos in liquid nitrogen was the geneticist breeders' solution to veterinary restrictions on the movement of live cattle across borders, with the bonus of being able to breed up to 60 calves in separate receiver cattle from just one flushed cow's uterus. I could see the economic appeal, to Wiechmann at least. He was not so much farming cattle as their uteri.

I thought back wistfully to my encounter with ubaba Mchunu in KwaZulu-Natal, whom we met in Chapter Two. Mchunu had explained that in his homestead, cattle were valued not just for what they could provide in milk, ploughing, calves and meat, but also for the multi-dimensional role they played in his household's spiritual life. Wiechmann must have sensed something in my expression:

Don't get me wrong. It is hard sometimes for me to slaughter a cow. You've known them for fifteen years. That cow has treated you very well, you get a personal relationship with it, and now it is old and must be slaughtered. It is hardest with the cattle we use for embryo flushing. Those cows we give names. And as soon as

they have a name, they are more special. They know your voice
… But ja … business is business.

The Wiechmann's farm was large, 10 000 hectares in all, and he farmed yet more land on lease. Wiechmann's herd, divided into stud and commercial, was 1 300 strong when I visited. He reckoned that was just about big enough.

Wiechmann hung onto his heifers, intending them either for embryo flushing or receiving. The commercial herd's bulls, however, were mostly castrated and sold from the age of two, mostly to the Meat Corporation of Namibia (Meatco).

Wiechmann also exported some calves as weaners to South African feedlots, although at a smaller scale than in the past because of the Namibian government's efforts to reduce the country's live export trade to its southern neighbour – ostensibly to bolster the national economy, although its 30% stake in Meatco certainly also plays a role. The problem for the Namibian government, however, comes when this vested interest runs counter to the direction of the maize price. When the harvest is bad and maize is expensive, feedlots reduce their activities; there is less South African demand for Namibian livestock and Meatco's supplies are good. But when the rains are good and the maize price is low, South African feedlot owners can afford more feed, and come rushing with hard-to-resist cash offers for Namibian cattle to fill their lots.

When cattle change hands in Southern Africa, there is a good chance it will involve an auction – our next stop along the cattle supply chain.

The auction house

A cattle auction is a revealing entrepôt, where subsistence farming meets commercial enterprise, and where feedlots and ancestral herds collide.

Rolf Aadnesgaard, a ruddy-faced, good-humoured white man in his fifties, has run an auction house since 2004. In the heat, a fitting description of Aadnesgaard borrows from the phrase King Shaka used in the 1820s, when he foresaw the arrival of men with ondlebe zibomvu, or 'red ears'. Aadnesgaard's red ears are matched by his hair. In his hometown, he is known as Jamludi, meaning 'red like wild beetroot'.

Aadnesgaard's grandparents are buried in Qhudeni near Nkandla, the KwaZulu-Natal site of former president Jacob Zuma's infamous homestead. Both his mother and father were born there, too – he of missionary stock and she the daughter of a local storekeeper and farmer. Aadnesgaard was born there, but the family had to relocate in the 1970s, when Qhudeni was declared part of a homeland. Today, Aadnesgaard lives with his wife, a beef farmer's daughter, in the KwaZulu-Natal Midlands.

> I don't do the auctioneering, but I hire the auctioneers. I organise the concert and they sing. We move about 1 000 head a week.

In Aadnesgaard's experience, commercial farmers sell cattle all the time. Mostly, they sell weaners – young cattle of about 10 months old that have only recently been weaned from their mothers:

> Your commercial farmer is always trying to maximise his kilos of beef per hectare. He will try to sell his weaners and get them as heavy as possible before the sale because he is paid by the kilo. Or else he will sell his cull cows, which are cows that haven't fallen in calf or are at the end of the road and are too old to conceive.

A 500-strong commercial herd contains 200 female weaners, but as Aadnesgaard points out, not all of these will fall pregnant:

> It does not take rocket science to know that some of these need to come out of the production line. So he [the farmer] will maybe get rid of 80 of the older girls.

The pre-auction process is a simple one: Aadnesgaard's field officers visit commercial farmers to discuss which cattle might sell and for what price. The farmer selects between 80 and 100 head of cattle, which the officer then photographs and posts on a website ahead of the auction.

Things do not run quite so straightforwardly with emerging farmers, according to Aadnesgaard:

> With the emerging guy you can't go along there and ask if he wants to sell. No. We tried that. It doesn't work. When he wants to sell he will bring that animal to your auction. There is no point going to him. We just need him to know when the auction is happening.

And when emerging farmers do sell, Aadnesgaard says, they typically do not sell weaners:

> For those guys to have an acclimatised weaner, one that can handle all the ticks and diseases of their area, well … that's huge. Instead, if they must, they sell their males, or whatever is of least value … In my experience, the black guys sell one cow at a time. It is very seldom otherwise.

Later, when I visited a commercial feedlot, this trend was confirmed: the feedlot claimed that only about 10% to 15% of cattle it purchased came from subsistence farmers from communal areas, with the rest still sourced from mainly white commercial farmers.

Aadnesgaard himself mostly sells to feedlots, which we discuss in greater detail in the next section. These send people to assess the weight and age of the animals on auction and bid on those that fit within the required parameters. This is in sharp contrast to the buyers wanting cattle for lobola:

> Let's say father-in-law has given you a deadline. He might even be there with you at the auction, saying, 'That one.' But there are three other fathers-in-law there too, all pointing at the same animal. And that means the price, if it's a good-looking heifer, will go through the roof. The feedlots don't stand a chance.

A heifer is a young female that has not yet borne a calf, meaning her fertile years lie before her, making her highly attractive for any homestead.

The feedlot

Karan Beef in Heidelberg, near Johannesburg, is the largest feedlot in Africa, supplying over a third of the national beef market. The company, which was taken over by the Public Investment Corporation and Pelo Agricultural Ventures in October 2018 for R5.2 billion, has over 140 000 head of cattle and onsite facilities that slaughter 2 000 cattle and debone 120 tonnes of meat *a day*.

When I visited, I was met at the gates by uniformed, Sotho-speaking security guards with clipboards and forms to complete. After calling the office to check I had an appointment, they waved me through.

Inside, I drove past mountains of hay bales, all neatly stacked to one side, with a sign saying, 'Please respect our biosecurity'. On the other side was an office complex, painted orange. The boss's parking place was reserved with a licence plate that simply said, 'BEEF 1'. Beyond that, stretching for acre after dusty acre, were the cattle pens.

There was no grass here, just earthen fields, fences, food troughs, dust, the odd vehicle driving around, and thousands and thousands of cattle. In marked contrast to the social, even chatty family-owned cattle I had met at the family homesteads in northern KwaZulu-Natal, here the cattle just stood around in the mud, looking bored, waiting for their next fix of feed.

A portly Afrikaans man from the company's research and development department arrived to show me around in his bakkie. When he said 'huge' – one of his favourite words – he took his time. *Huuuuuge*.

In the old days, all the beef in South Africa was veld-fed. The cattle were slaughtered at three, four, even six years old. I remember as a young boy in the 1960s, the meat was tough, with yellow fat, and not so nice.

In this man's telling of it, a consumer revolt during the mid-1960s ended in the country increasingly turning away from the chewy meat of older cattle in favour of younger, more tender beef. Agricultural researchers then found that for maximum tenderness, you need to slaughter cattle before their permanent teeth emerge, at about 12 to 14 months old.

Of course, cattle that young still have a lot of growing to do. Slaughtering them at that age means commercial and communal farmers – who get paid by the kilogram – miss out on revenue they would have received if they had waited for the animals to beef up some more. And so South Africa's feedlots were born.

> You take a calf away from his mother at weaning and start feeding him high-density rations. You pen him, you put him in a feedlot. You will get faster growth and an animal with a better finish and you can slaughter him earlier.

Feedlots typically offer farmers a higher price for weaners than for older animals to factor in anticipated future growth. In this way, the expected future profit from the cattle's fattening is split with the breeding farmers, tempting them into the market. Said the Karan Beef manager:

> We try to pay the lowest price to farmers, but even so studies show the beef farmer gets 40% of the amount the consumer pays. That's much higher than a dairy or maize farmer.

Stuffing weaners with high-density feed reliably delivers tender meat – and plenty of it. Plus, it turns out, there is another 'advantage': white fat. In the 1960s, South African meat buyers started following the European and American trend of viewing white fat as healthier and somehow better than yellow fat, despite the fact that cattle fat is naturally yellow if she has – as nature intended – been eating grass. According to Karan Beef's representative:

The way to turn cattle fat from yellow to white is to keep them off pasture and give them maize. It takes up to five weeks for a young calf, and three months for an old one.

Part of the push for feedlots in the United States, where they began, was that they were profitable places to send that country's massive maize surplus. American feedlotted cattle are so richly fed that they produce more fat than they can store under their skins, in the subcutaneous fat layer. This results in excess fat being deposited between their muscle fibres, creating what the meat industry calls marbling. At slaughter, in a process known as hot carcass trimming, American feedlotted cattle's subcutaneous fat deposits are sliced off and discarded. For a time, these deposits were also, problematically, fed back to the cattle.

South African feedlots, though in general enthusiastic disciples of the American way, have never had the luxury of excess maize. The country is prone to drought and rarely generates massive, cut-price maize surpluses. So feedlots, though born of an American model, have adjusted. As the Karan Beef manager recalls:

> We in South Africa decided not to go the marbling route. Our maize is just too expensive and the consumer won't pay. So the buyers had to get used to lean beef with a nice layer of fat on the outside.

Conveniently for the industry, the South Africa Meat Industry Company (SAMIC), which is licensed by the Department of Agriculture, Forestry and Fisheries to grade beef, has lent a helping classificatory hand. Where the United States Department of Agriculture (USDA) gives a prime grading to beef 'produced from young, well-fed beef cattle [with] abundant marbling', SAMIC awards an A-grade (or, as SAMIC insists, an A 'classification') to beef from cattle with no permanent incisors, in other words, to cattle under the age of 14 months. SAMIC awards a '1' to beef with a slender column of subcutaneous fat, and a '2' and '3' for fattier beef. There is no mention of marbling.

The happy consequence of the USDA and SAMIC systems, for both American and South African feedlots, is that their mainstream outputs score the best grades in both systems. According to a senior SAMIC official:

> South African meat-eaters want tenderness. So we classify the meat on that. We don't judge the colour of the fat, though it is true that meat-eaters here are now used to white fat. People want a bit of fat, though. It is good on a braai … The most popular categories are A2 and A3. About 88% of our meat is A2 or A3.

Observing that the grading makes no reference to taste, I asked whether SAMIC's classification was really consumer-driven. The official conceded:

> In truth, it is more industry- than public-driven. That is what the industry wants to produce. We can't produce more hectares of farmland, so the answer is to have more cattle per hectare. And that points to feedlots.

The case against feedlots

Feedlotted cattle in the United States are fed maize – maize that could, detractors say, be better used to directly meet the nutritional needs of humans. This is not entirely true in South Africa, where feedlot cattle are fed 'hominy chop', a blend of by-products from the production of cottonseed, soy and maize meal that is not fit for human consumption. The Karan Beef manager put it this way:

> For many years, people ate maize meal that was milled on farms. Every little dorpie had a mill. And they didn't refine that maize. I can remember mealie pap from my young days and it is not like the pap you get today. There was way more of the grit of the maize they left in there. And then people didn't want to eat the yellow mealie pap. No. It had to be white. So they started taking out the starch too, just refining it more and more. Now … where

is all that by-product, what we call hominy chop, going to go? I will tell you … to our cattle.

Feeding cattle hominy chop might be better than giving them straight maize, but the basic question remains: rather than giving over large tracts of land to grow maize, would South Africa's limited agricultural land not be better used to produce a *variety* of crops to meet the country's nutritional needs?

Feedlotted cattle also produce large amounts of manure. I had been expecting to find fetid piles of the stuff at Karan Beef, but when I got there, the farm didn't smell much at all. This is because local small-scale farmers buy the manure, using it on their fields to enrich the soil. Said the Karan Beef manager:

> If we go the first-world way and build a biogas plant like the Europeans want, and turn all our manure into energy, I dread to think of how these farmers will react. That really will create a huge stink.

It seems an elegant, African solution to the problem, but it still leaves the question of methane – a potent greenhouse gas and contributor to climate breakdown. Most bovine methane emissions originate not from manure or flatulence, as one might assume, but from burping. The Karan Beef manager claimed that his grain-fed cattle gave off far less methane than pasture-fed cattle. Even if this is true, feedlots increase the land's capacity for cattle, and more cattle equals more burps, which equals more methane. The methane emissions from mega-feedlots like Karan Beef are a major environmental hazard, and, I believe, constitute a powerful reason for doing away with feedlots altogether – but more on that in Chapter Eight.

Another argument against feedlots is this: despite their four stomachs, cattle struggle to digest grain, which is low in fibre compared to grass. As in humans, fibre plays a role in digestive health by keeping food moving through and out of the digestive system. Without enough fibre bulk to move things along, grain hangs around longer in the bovine digestive system, producing fermentation acids and generally making the animal susceptible to infection. So what on earth are we doing taking them off grass and feeding them a grain-based diet? The feedlots' answer is that the cattle get fatter more quickly. According to the Karan Beef manager:

> As soon as you start pushing the envelope in terms of what the cattle eat, you start to get disorders. That is a major focus for us here ... finding the precise point where you cannot cross. Because you need to maximise and you need to optimise ...
>
> Lung infection is a major issue. Twenty percent of our cattle have it in winter, though it goes down in summer. But there is a big immunity challenge on the feedlot. We treat them and re-treat them with antibiotics, but they still get infected. It's because the cattle are in such close contact with each other.

Twenty percent of a herd with lung infections is huge. *Huuuuuge.* By way of comparison, one farmer with pasture-fed cattle I spoke to said a 1% sickness rate would be high for his herd. Despite the high sickness rate, the Karan Beef manager reckoned the cattle mortality rate was only 1%, at most. This is because feedlots slaughter their cattle before they get too sick.

According to the World Health Organization (WHO), this endless injection and re-injection of feedlotted cattle with antibiotics is hastening the emergence of mutated, drug-resistant microbacteria, which reduces the effectiveness of antibiotics for both livestock and people. So much so, in fact, that in 2017 the WHO recommended that farmers stop using antibiotics to promote growth and prevent disease in healthy animals.

Feedlot cattle are not just up to their horns in antibiotics. They are also given synthetic growth hormones, implanted as slow-release pellets under the skin of the animal's ear. And muscle growth enhancers. And ionophor, to improve the animals' ability to absorb nutrients, which also acts as an antibiotic. Even though the European Union has banned the use of some hormones, the manager was unapologetic:

> We have no qualms about using these hormones. We know they
> are safe. All that stuff that your teenaged daughter will grow
> boobs this size and the boys' testicles will shrink and all that
> shit … there is no clinical evidence. It is just impossible with the
> hormone dosages we work with. If you ate 75 kilos of our beef
> every day you would end up with the same level of hormones as
> are in your body already.

He was thankful that the South African government took a more
sympathetic stance:

> In South Africa, our government has given us the leniency to use
> these products. We tend to follow the American FDA [Food and
> Drug Administration] system, rather than the European GAP
> [Good Agricultural Practices]. The difference is that FDA has
> 'minimum levels' for everything. There is always a minimum
> residue level that is acceptable. GAP has no [minimum] levels.
> But never say never. Our government recently followed GAP on
> bovine spongiform encephalopathy, BSE, which you would know
> as mad cow disease, rather than the FDA. So we are watching
> carefully and taking nothing for granted.

The bottom line, said the manager, was that hormones put an extra
10% growth on cattle, which means feedlots can sell beef for a few
rands less per kilo. Hormone-free beef would sell at a rate not many
retailers are willing to pay because, the manager said, few South
Africans care whether their beef has hormones or not.

For Wiechmann, the Namibian cattle farmer, hormone use was
one of the key differences between beef from his country and from
South Africa:

> Look … we can't use growth hormones, which they use a lot in
> South Africa. We are exporting to the EU market, and they don't

allow hormones and stuff like that. South African meat is filled with things Europeans don't want to touch. The Europeans get our best meat cuts. The rest we sell to South Africa.

Selling to Europe, he said, is lucrative but exacting:

> Everything must be packaged in a certain way. And the packaging is expensive. There is a certain size of box, and your sirloin must fit perfectly into it. It must be one piece. The box goes to the pallet, which goes to the container. Every square centimetre is used. It is easier to do this if the carcasses are larger, and it looks better on display. There must be not too much fat, but there must be marbling. That is not a typical African trait, but our genetics work sees to that.

In South Africa, most people just want a steady supply of the cheapest beef possible. And this, the Karan Beef manager said, means feedlots.

> If you want to feed 50 million or so South Africans, of which about half are eating beef, there is no way you can do that from pasture ... it would take a farm the size of the Free State.

South Africa simply doesn't have enough suitable grazing land available. According to the manager:

> Our pastures simply cannot handle these stock densities. There are a few areas in our country, like the KwaZulu-Natal Midlands, that have rainfall and good grass and you can keep stock in huge numbers. But if the grazing is out in Vryburg or the Kalahari or somewhere ... no way. You will need 20 hectares per animal in those places, though it is about half on the savanna.

The national Department of Agriculture, Forestry and Fisheries confirms this, with its official recommendation being 6 hectares per animal on grassland, 12 hectares per animal on savanna, and 25 hectares per animal in arid areas like the Karoo. The country's total cattle population – including subsistence herds, which are estimated to account for about half the cattle – is about 14 million strong. Using an average of 12 hectares per cow, it would take 168 million hectares to support this population. From end to end, South Africa is only 122 million hectares big – and only a small portion of it is suitable for grazing. That means that if all our beef was grass fed, there would be no way the country could sustain a cattle population of this size – or supply enough beef to sate existing demand in the local market. This is often taken as an argument in favour of feedlots, though it is also a powerful part of the case for reducing our beef consumption.

The final argument against feedlots is aesthetic. The beef that Karan and other South African feedlots produce by the tonne is undoubtedly tender, as befits meat from animals that haven't even cut their permanent teeth. But what does it taste like? In my experience, the rural KwaZulu-Natal farmers are right – the meat is basically flavourless. Perhaps this is why beef is so often served drenched in a sauce so pungent that even the most flavourful flesh would struggle to penetrate it.

The abattoir

The National Party, which ruled South Africa from 1948 until 1994, was largely delivered to power by the votes of Afrikaans farmers and particularly those who were struggling to make ends meet. One of the main nightmares of this constituency was the bottom falling out of the market, whether it was for beef, maize or milk, leaving them unable to service their loans and thus putting their farms at risk. To protect these farmers from such a fate and at the same time to extend its own influence over agriculture, the National Party introduced state-owned and controlled marketing boards for all the main agricultural commodities. One of these was the South African Meat Board.

The Meat Board decreed that farmers could no longer slaughter at home where there were no government inspectors on hand, but instead must transport their livestock to government-designated abattoirs to meet their Maker. Every municipality had its own state-owned abattoir – Maitland in Cape Town, City Deep in Johannesburg and so on – and it was illegal to slaughter anywhere else if the meat was destined for the market. More than this, farmers needed permits from the Board for permission to slaughter at its abattoirs. Largely excluded from the system were subsistence farmers, who were permitted to slaughter at home without a licence, provided they did not sell the meat in town. The Board charged a levy on each animal slaughtered, and the money was pooled into a fund that was used to implement a pricing floor. The system meant that even if the meat price dropped below a certain level, the Board still paid farmers the floor price, easing their free market nightmares.

When the ANC government took over in 1994 it felt no political obligation to protect white commercial farmers and moved swiftly to weaken state control of the sector, breaking up the agricultural marketing boards and abolishing the price floor system. Also abolished were the tight controls on where animals could be slaughtered. Now farmers could apply for individual slaughter licences from the Ministry of Agriculture. The result was an increase in competition for state-owned abattoirs – for which, after years of monopoly, the abattoirs were ill-prepared.

One of the best-performing new abattoirs is Tomis, in the Western Cape. I visited Tomis one clouded, autumnal day. The abattoir, which has a feedlot attached, is up the West Coast from Cape Town, near enough that you can still see the hazy outline of Table Mountain. Several Nguni hides were tied to a barbed-wire fence near the entrance, apparently on sale though no one emerged to sell them. Beyond them, guarded by cypress trees, were three ancient graves. Not far off was a modest wooden-slatted house, a Western Cape Stormers flag flying from the stoep. An elderly woman came out and waved us up the track towards an office building and, right next door, the abattoir.

After a brief wait, we were ushered into the office of Laurie

Terblanche. Though young, Terblanche was broad in stature and evidently a man who liked his meat.

Tomis, Terblanche told me, started in the mid-1990s when Terblanche's stepfather and mother, Tom and Isabelle – hence the name Tomis – bought a farm with a permit to slaughter five to 10 sheep per day. It was not long before a Muslim-owned meat wholesaler approached Tomis and asked if the abattoir would consider halaal slaughter.

> It was a bit weird for us. It really was the new South Africa. We didn't know what to expect ... We are from a conservative background ... but so are they. We have found that if we respect them, they will respect us.

Originally dealing exclusively in lamb, Tomis began slaughtering beef in the early 2000s after seeing that Cape Town's massive Maitland abattoir, filled with old machinery and lacking the funds to refurbish, had become increasingly unable to compete. The entry of new players like Tomis hastened Maitland's demise, and the old abattoir finally closed its doors in 2005. More recently, life has become harder for would-be new entrants into the abattoir game, primarily, it seems, due to tightened health and safety requirements, which have caused compliance costs to soar. But when Tomis first opened its doors, the market was ripe for the taking.

By the time of my visit, Tomis was slaughtering 120 cattle a day, with two teams constantly on the go. Some of the cattle were slaughtered on contract; the rest had been purchased from farms and auctions. Unlike in the United States, where journalists and animal rights activists have had to resort to devious means to get into abattoirs, Terblanche was happy for us to look round. Cattle were milling around in an outside pen, aware that something was up, but not looking too stressed. These were steered, one by one, up onto a narrow ramp with chest-high metal walls. A uniformed worker dabbed a liquid onto their foreheads.

As each new animal clattered onto the ramp, the ones at the front were pushed forward. The cow at the front soon found itself up against a wall with a large hole at head height. A gate was slid between the cow's rear and the muzzle of the animal behind. A moment later, when the cow confusedly stuck its head through the hole, a second uniformed worker pressed a stun gun to the cow's forehead where the liquid had been rubbed, and pulled the trigger. There was a clunk from the gun and a moan from the cow, which sank to its knees. The cow was quickly lifted off the ramp and slung on a hook by its hind legs. Two workers, dressed in green plastic pinafores to protect their clothes from blood, then quickly slit the stunned cow's throat, killing it – instantly, they claimed. A conveyor belt then swung the hooked-up carcass forward a short distance so that it hung over a metal basin to catch the blood gushing from its neck.

Meanwhile, there was another clunk of the stun gun. Another moan. More falling to the knees. Another sequence of grabbing, hooking and slicing. More blood. After the bloodletting was done, each carcass jolted from the sink to a section where men washed them down and skinned them. Before long, these carcasses would be hanging from more hooks, this time in refrigerated trucks, ready to hit the roads to Cape Town's supermarkets and meat wholesalers.

The abattoirs in the literature of American animal rights activists are mostly blood-spattered hell-holes where thousands of stressed-out cattle are slaughtered at breakneck speed every day. There are, according to the activists who have investigated them, many equally gruesome abattoirs in South Africa, with poorly paid and trained workers slaughtering cattle in unsavoury and cruel conditions. At Tomis, however, the pace of cattle slaughter is unhurried. Its management is happy for me to view operations because they genuinely reckon their setup is okay.

Tomis abattoir has passed official inspection – many times. But an abattoir is still an abattoir. It is still an industrialised killing floor. Even without unnecessary cruelty, the clinical nature with which death is dispensed at Tomis remains jarringly at odds with the gentle nature of the cattle being slaughtered. The only notable consolation is that the deaths of the cattle arrived so quickly, that there did not seem enough time for panic to set in, and the set-up was arranged such that the cattle could not witness the death of others before they too received the stun gun's blast.

Across South Africa's border, in Eswatini, abattoirs face a different challenge: the scarcity of cattle to slaughter. On a trip there I met with Tim R ('you don't need to know my surname'), an elderly white man running an abattoir in Phuzumoya, a small, modest lowveld town, who for decades has supplied ration meat for workers at the Swazi lowveld sugar factories. Tim said things in his business were changing for the better:

These days, the workers want fair quality rations. And fair enough. We try to give them that now. Twenty years ago, you could give them anything and we did ... I feel a bit guilty about that.

Tim's voice trailed off, and there was a brief pause before he resumed.

I buy my cattle from all over Swaziland. I buy from African farmers. I've been doing it for 30 years. And in all that time it has been the same. No one ever wants to sell. It is always as a last resort, to pay for something. At this time of year, January, there is a big flood of cattle on the market because of schools opening. People need to pay school fees. The cycle is always the same.

Tim manages to source a few extra cattle from commercial farmers but faces many hurdles. Not only is the already small number of commercial farmers in the country steadily falling, but he is facing increased competition from Swazi cattle speculators for cattle from the Swazi Nation Lands:

In the old days, there were very few cattle buyers. I used to go to the dips to buy and I could buy 15 animals at a time. Now, it's not just the old white guys like me who are in the business. The Africans are doing it too. There are many, many buyers now.

In Eswatini and back in South Africa, the big buying from abattoirs is done by meat wholesalers, who in turn supply supermarkets and superettes the length and breadth of the country.

The wholesaler

The democratisation of South Africa and the subsequent liberalisation of the agricultural sector affected not only abattoirs but also wholesalers. Before 1994, the wholesale meat trade was dominated by a somewhat complacent handful of white-owned players. Today, this has largely changed, with numerous black players entering the ring, particularly in the country's major cities.

In Cape Town, the two big players before 1994 were Vleissentraal and Karoo. These days, according to Terblanche from Tomis:

It is the Muslim guys who sell the most meat and dominate the wholesale trade. You would be surprised at how much they do.

One of the biggest meat wholesalers in Cape Town is Airport Meats, whose founders and owners are the Parkers, a coloured Muslim family from Rondebosch East. I met the company's chief executive, Seraaj Parker, at the company's offices near Cape Town International Airport. He was seated next to a tapestry with an extract from the Qur'an and a statue with the inscription, 'Palestine – thank you'.

Parker told me that Airport Meats got its break when the government scrapped the rule that only municipal-owned abattoirs could slaughter:

The market opened up. We found we could buy meat from abattoirs outside of Cape Town for far cheaper than the government-owned Maitland abattoir could supply. It just couldn't compete.

Being a Muslim company in Cape Town definitely has its advantages, Parker said:

Most of the meat retailers in town are halaal. So naturally they want a wholesaler who is halaal too. Otherwise you can get contamination.

Inaccurate or fake halaal meat certification has been a worry for the South African Muslim community for years, particularly after a scandal in 2011 when Orion, one of the largest meat wholesalers in the country, was accused of knowingly labelling kangaroo, water buffalo and – worse – pork, as halaal. The company alleged sabotage. To provide peace of mind to Muslim consumers, in December 2018 Shabeer Shaik Adburahman, a specialist in Islamic finances, launched a new decentralised application that used blockchain to digitally encrypt and verify halaal certificates. Similar systems already exist in other parts of the world, including the United Kingdom and Dubai.

Parker said that of all the meats, beef was the most profitable to wholesale, mostly because the wholesaler's margin – at between 25% and 30% – is far higher on beef than on other meats. With lamb, for example, wholesalers mark up the abattoir price by just 10%. Precisely because beef trades at such a premium, Parker cautioned shoppers to be particularly wary of cut-price wors:

If it is really so cheap, then you have to wonder why. My rule is that if I wouldn't eat it, I won't sell it.

The retailer

After being distributed by meat wholesalers, most beef ends up in a familiar location: the supermarket.

On a scorchingly hot afternoon during late summer, I met Donovan Hayes, the general manager of a large supermarket chain's butcheries, and his team. Selling directly to consumers, Hayes and his team are well placed to detect buying trends, including increases in demand for compassionately reared, free-range or grass-fed beef. According to Hayes and his team, people are increasingly concerned about the conditions animals live in and what they eat – but only when it comes to poultry and pigs. This increase in consumer compassion does not, they claimed, extend to larger livestock – possibly because few people are aware that cattle and sheep are 'finished' in feedlots. Said the manager:

> With cattle and sheep, most South Africans still think of them as being basically free range, and either don't know or aren't bothered that they are finished off in a feedlot before slaughter.

According to the supermarket buyers, the main problem with grass-fed beef is inconsistent quality. High-quality grass-fed beef depends on high-quality grazing, and in South Africa, good grass is in short supply. By comparison, feedlotted beef is reliably tender, even if it is tasteless.

Another problem, mentioned earlier, is that grass-fed beef has yellow fat, which urban meat consumers tend to understand as meaning the meat is not fresh. Consumers are wrong about this, just as they are wrong in thinking that bright red beef is better than darker slices (darker steaks are older, and steak improves with age). But supermarkets feel obliged to give the public what it wants. And rather than educate the public about yellow fat, supermarket butchers keep sourcing and selling white-fatted beef.

Which is not to say that South African consumers turn their noses up at anything but the best-quality meat (however they understand this to be determined). Faced with rapidly rising prices, South African consumers tend to turn to less expensive types of meat like chicken, polony and viennas to maintain meat volume rather than buying less meat.

The local word polony (or French polony, as it is often inexplicably called) is derived from the Italian city of Bologna, but the product is a far cry from the city's mortadella sausage on which it is allegedly modelled. A mortadella sausage is – or should be – a fine thing, made from top-quality pork mixed with small cubes of lard.

Local polony should contain at least 75% meat or 'meat equivalent'. A key ingredient of polony, viennas and other meat products reassuringly labelled '100% beef' – like burger patties – is LFTB and its poultry-based equivalent, mechanically deboned meat. Imported mechanically deboned meat is widely suspected of being behind a deadly outbreak of listeriosis in South Africa in 2018, which killed over 200 people. The meat responsible for the outbreak was traced to a cold meats factory in Limpopo, and then on to Brazil. Although the Brazilian meat industry has hotly denied that its exports were responsible for the listeriosis outbreak, Brazilian police have reported finding that five laboratories there allegedly falsified results of meat-sample tests from the national poultry giant BRF, apparently to hide poor sanitary conditions and a high incidence of *Salmonella*.

Some might find it reassuring that boerewors, another low-cost beef steak substitute, is not allowed to include offal or mechanically deboned meat. Technically, boerewors must be 90% meat. However, that still leaves a hefty 10% legally reserved for spices and unspecified 'other' ingredients. And while most of the meat is beef, with the balance made up of lamb or pork, outside of supermarkets anything can happen and it is not uncommon to find donkey, buffalo or other meat sources in the mix.

The cattle in the commercial beef supply chain lead short lives with every phase of life optimised with the bottom line in mind. Dairy farming, while also profit-driven, has a reputation for being a softer type of cattle farming simply because the cows live longer. In the next chapter, we examine the dairy commercial complex, and whether their longer lifespan goes hand in hand with a happier, healthier life for dairy cows.

CHAPTER FIVE

Milking it: the relentless growth of dairy

Catching many consumers unawares, South Africa experienced a serious butter shortage during 2017. Not only were the shelves often empty of the precious stuff, but when it was available, butter sold for eye-watering prices. The butter price had risen nearly a third from its 2016 level. One of the reasons for the butter shortage, according to some media pundits, was the Banting diet, which advocates, among other things, the guilt-free use of liberal quantities of full-cream milk and butter. It was Banting-inspired demand for butter and cream, the theory went, that pushed South African butter demand beyond the available supply.

Inconveniently, the statistics show that national butter consumption is not rising but is instead (slightly) falling. However, this seems less likely to be because of lower demand nationally – though rising prices are an increasing deterrent for many hard-pressed South African shoppers – and more because of an increasingly tightened supply of butter, both domestically and internationally. Butter supply has tightened globally in part because of growing consumer demand for full-cream milk, which leaves less cream available to make butter. Another factor is rising international demand for butter, which has outstripped global supply growth and has slashed the world's once-enormous butter reserves. The famed European Union butter mountain, for example, weighed over 92 000 tonnes in mid-2016 but had shrunk to a small hillock of just 1 369 tonnes a year later. Inevitably, there has been a steep increase in the international spot price for butter, which climbed from US$ 3 485 per tonne in January 2015 to US$ 5 544 per tonne in April 2019, with some severe price spikes in between. More steep price increases seem inevitable going forward, driven by growth in international demand that seems likely to continue to exceed supply.

In line with these international trends, South African dairy consumption as a whole is on the up. In fact, South Africans seem to love their dairy even more than they love their beef. In 2016, the average South African ate or drank 58 kg of dairy products, compared to a recorded 45 kg in 2005, an increase of 29%.

The greatest increase in consumption was in processed milk, both because new farming techniques are increasing yield and because the unit price has remained relatively flat compared to other dairy products, encouraging consumers across the board to add more milk to their diets.

The second-biggest consumption increase was in yoghurts, a category that lumps together the type of yoghurt most Western consumers are familiar with – that is, milk that has been fermented with added bacteria and then sweetened and flavoured – and amasi, or, in Afrikaans, maas.

Like yoghurt, amasi is also fermented milk. However, rather than adding specific bacteria, traditional amasi is made by simply storing unpasteurised cow's milk in a calabash or sack until it naturally separates out into a watery whey, called umlaza in Zulu, and the sourish curds of amasi. The whey is often discarded, though it can be used to reconstitute fruit juices and as a starter culture when fermenting vegetables. Amasi can be eaten on its own but is more commonly mixed with maize meal, or pap, to make a porridge. To the dismay and disgust of purists, some people – especially the youth – also mix amasi with sugar.

South Africa's main dairies manufacture their own versions of amasi, adding microbial organisms that produce lactic acid to get the milk fermenting rather than relying on natural fermentation. Sacrilege, perhaps, but at least – unlike most yoghurts – commercially manufactured amasi has no added preservatives, and there does seem to be an effort to reproduce, more or less, the sour taste and texture of traditional amasi.

The drought that ravaged the northern and eastern parts of the country in 2015 and 2016, and had the Western Cape in its grip until good rains finally fell there in mid-2018, gently reversed the previously relentless rise in domestic milk production, which increased from about 2 billion litres in 2006 to 3.1 billion litres by 2016, falling back about 6% to about 2.9 billion litres in 2017. To the relief of dairy farmers, who have complained for years that the milk price was too low, the drought years nudged raw (unprocessed and unpasteurised) milk prices upwards. Yet with the national economy in the doldrums and consumers' purchasing power diminished, people's ability to pay more for dairy products is tightly constrained, putting pressure on retailers to keep milk prices from skyrocketing.

To achieve this, retailers have driven hard bargains with dairies, which are at the same time faced with strongly increasing input costs. The result is that dairy profits are mostly falling.

The big dairy debate: grass-fed versus mixed rations farming

Recent butter trends aside, at first sight it seems odd that the increase in national dairy consumption has not been matched by an increase in the number of dairy farms. There are thought to be about 4 300 dairy farmers in South Africa, which is a hefty 39% less than in 1997, when there were 7 077. Most dairy farmers are in the country's coastal areas, from the Western Cape West Coast, all the way around to KwaZulu-Natal. The Western and Eastern Capes and KwaZulu-Natal contribute 78% of national commercial dairy production between them, while the Free State contributes a further 10%. Despite there being fewer farmers, South Africa's milk production has risen by 50% over the past decade. What happened?

For one thing, the size of dairy herds has been growing. According to a 1995 study by the Western Cape Department of Agriculture, 58%

of milk producers in the province produced less than 500 litres a day, but fewer than 1% produced more than 3 000 litres. By 2004, only 23% of dairy farmers produced less than 500 litres a day, while 21% produced more than 3 000 litres. Small-scale producers generated 19% of total recorded milk production in 1995 but only 6% in 2004.

One dairy farmer who is living proof of this trend is Simon Matthews, a fourth-generation cattle farmer and owner of a dairy farm called Glendye in Alexandria, a lush, water-blessed part of the Eastern Cape between Port Elizabeth and Port Alfred. Matthews' father started farming in 1981 and made a good living from 151 cows. Today – without the protections of government subsidies and historical trade restrictions on dairy imports, and coupled with a market dominated by large retailers that use their immense buying power to drive milk prices down despite production costs going up – Matthews said he needs a thousand cows, nearly seven times as many as his father, to maintain the same standard of living.

Matthews' pasture was lush, his fences in order, and his milking facilities immaculate. The place hummed with activity. Matthews was modest about his role, ascribing his success to the farm's location:

This area is blessed with some of the best rainfall in South Africa. So we actually have grass, unlike many farms in the country. The basis of our cows' diet is grass, but when we are short we use silage, and a maize concentrate.

Matthews' herd used to be mainly Friesian, whose milk is said to be perfect for the low-fat final product. But because of growing consumer taste for creamier milk, Matthews has increasingly shifted to Jerseys.

As with most dairy farms, and contrary to the popular image of cattle lowing contentedly in pasture, the cows at Glendye cannot roam freely. Instead, they are in a feedlot. Said Matthews:

All their food is brought to them. But at least it isn't like in the Western Cape and other drier places, where they go for the total mix ration system. At least there is plenty of grass in the mix here.

Total mix ration, or TMR, is a blend of grasses, grains and supplements designed to boost milk production in cows. Dairy farmers – especially those in drier areas, like the Western Cape – use TMR to get more milk from their cattle. But this places a heavy burden on the cows themselves:

> When a cow calves, she lactates for 300 days. After that we give her a 60-day rest before we impregnate her again. Our cows last about six to seven years, and we usually get three to four lactations out of them.
>
> We milk our cows twice a day, and we get around 17 litres a day. The TMR farmers can get 30 to 35 litres. But then, their cattle often only get two lactations, and last only two years.

Matthews told me he loved cattle and enjoyed the challenge of the business side of things. But now that his herd was much bigger than it used to be, there were aspects of the old ways that he missed:

> I used to know all my cows. I recognised their udders – not surprising, I suppose, since I mostly see them from behind. But when you go over 600 cattle, they move from being individuals to numbers. I'm sorry to say, but I'm not intrigued by their individuality any more.

Matthews had painted a somewhat bleak picture of TMR dairies, complete with feed- and hormone-stuffed, stressed-out, short-lived cows. (Matthews himself said he did not use BST, or bovine somatotropin, a bovine growth hormone beloved of American dairies and approved by the FDA but abhorred by many out of concern for what it might be doing to people, and especially the young – although he told me there are others who say they don't use BST, but 'believe me, they do'.)

To get another perspective, I visited Johannes Loubser, the manager at the Fair Cape dairy on Kuiperskraal farm in Durbanville, Cape Town. Loubser, a jovial, ruddy-faced man, was also from a farming family – Johannes was the fifth generation of Loubsers to live on the farm. His children, he added, were the sixth. Kuiperskraal was once a wheat farm with a few sheep. Despite the lack of grass in fynbos-covered Durbanville, Loubser's father brought in cattle. By the mid-2010s, when I visited the farm, Loubser's herd numbered 1 400 and produced 50 000 litres a day.

Loubser's herd consists mostly of Friesians because they are, he said, better at handling a TMR diet. As Loubser put it:

> Our cows don't graze, because there ain't no grazing. This area turns into a desert between November and May. This is not a naturally good place for cows. It's a good place for us, though, because it's close to Cape Town.

Loubser insisted that TMR was 'good, healthy stuff':

> You can't give [the cows] rubbish or they aren't going to give you milk. They won't reproduce. We give them a mixture of hay and concentrates, lucerne and silage. We use maize meal, cottonseed and soya ...

Loubser dismissed the suggestion that giving cattle feed so different from their natural diet is asking for trouble:

> Today, we are not farming the cattle ... no. We are farming their rumens [their large first stomachs]. It is all about the rumen. And the rumen is very sensitive. It consists of two thirds of the cow's body weight. It makes up a huge part of the dairy cow, and that is where everything happens. Now ... if you have a healthy rumen, you will have milk, and you will have a happy cow. It's science.

So what did Loubser think about BST? Fair Cape doesn't use BST, but only because of market demands. He gave a chuckle:

> All over the world they have tried finding reasons why BST is bad for humans, but they cannot get one study to blame it for what is going on in our bodies.

I raised Matthews' point about TMR cattle being stressed and dying young. Loubser waved his hand impatiently and said that the Eastern Cape farmers don't know what they are talking about. He did admit that Eastern Cape cows last longer than those reared in the Western Cape, but maintained that life for Western Cape dairy cattle – and the quality of the milk they produce – has improved dramatically over the years:

> Look … the main thing you need to understand about dairy in this country is that the quality is 20 times better than before. Our factories are better. We are homogenising, pasteurising, clarifying … Our quality is unbelievable …
>
> At the same time, we are raising yields like you can't believe. My cows produce over 40 litres a day. Cows that produce 100 000 litres over their lifespan are coming through. Five years ago, that was like totally impossible. And now in my own herd I probably have 20 cows in the last year reaching 100 000 litres of milk. And that is going to double those figures in the next years to come. I can see it.

Along with rising herd numbers among those dairy farmers who have managed to stay in the game, this rising productivity in cows explains why the country's dairy production is increasing even as the number of farms are decreasing.

In support of emerging dairy farmers

The constant growth in the size of dairy farms has made it ever harder for new entrants, and particularly emerging black farmers, to gain a toehold in dairy farming. As Matthews pointed out:

> Emerging farmers today can get drought relief [from the state], but not much else … And the cost of entry just keeps rising. Let's say you have 300 cattle. These days it will cost you thirty, forty thousand per cow to get a dairy going. That's R10 million. Where is an emerging farmer going to get that? Commercial banks won't help.

For once, Loubser agreed:

> For a new dairy farmer to start from scratch today … I think it
> is impossible. He will not make it. Unless maybe there's foreign
> money involved, or it is subsidised. Look … to build a dairy like
> ours is R100 million and you haven't even bought the animals.
> My animals are worth another R40 million. So now that is R140
> million. Even if you have that kind of capital, how are you going
> to get enough return on it on the low margins we are running?
> More and more farmers will fail. I get an SMS every day about a
> dairy farm being sold. I got one this morning. I had one yesterday
> … They sell for dirt cheap and I don't want to buy them.

Matthews and Loubser are right. The cost of entering dairy farming has
risen relentlessly over the past 20 years, and the general perception in
the farming community is that funding – whether from the government
or commercial banks – is much too hard to come by.

This is the unpromising terrain in which the government is attempting
land reform. Despite the challenges, there are a few shining examples
of land reform and agricultural development that deserve mention.
One such story is that of Amadlelo Agri, which was established in
2004 to make use of under- or unused farmland and train communities
in commercial farming and management. Through the initiative,
Matthews and about 70 other white farmers from the Eastern Cape
and KwaZulu-Natal are working to develop community-owned farms
in the old Ciskei, in the hopes that this will help transform the South
African dairy industry.

Quietly, amid a stream of bad news about failed agricultural
empowerment projects, Amadlelo Agri is going strong. The white
farmers pay a portion of the farms' loans and supply equipment
and cattle, while the community provides the ground and labour.
The proceeds are then split 50/50. 'I think it's a good formula,' said
Matthews.

This type of farming, known as sharemilking, allows emerging farmers to enter dairy production even if they do not have the capital to buy cows and infrastructure. In total, Amadlelo milks 7 600 cattle in partnership with 300 people from local communities. The dairies – of which there are six – pay out around R17 million a year to local communities in wages and a further R15 million in dividends.

In contrast to the heartening tale of Amadlelo, one of the worst recent examples of the derailment of public resources meant for community empowerment also involves a dairy project, this time in Vrede in the north-eastern Free State. Vrede is a small farming town of around 20 000 people in the province's Thabo Mofutsanyana district, whose former mayor, Mosebenzi Zwane, went on to become the provincial Minister of Agriculture. It was in this position that Zwane signed off on a 2012 deal to give a company called Estina a free 99-year lease on a 4 400-hectare farm near Vrede, plus R114 million a year for three years, to establish a dairy for the benefit of emerging Vrede farmers.

It later emerged that Estina's director was Kamal Vasram, an IT salesman, not a farmer, while the company itself was a front for the infamous Gupta brothers, who will forever be known in South Africa's history for their alleged role in corrupting the country's highest officials and ruthlessly exploiting its resources through dodgy deals such as this one.

Estina was booted off the project in 2014 after an urgent investigation by the National Treasury, but not before the Free State government had paid the company R114 million – of which R30 million seems to have gone towards the lavish wedding of a Gupta niece in 2013.

When Ramaphosa became South Africa's president in early 2018, he swiftly booted Zwane – who was by then the Minister of Mineral Resources – from Cabinet. The National Prosecuting Authority (NPA) also moved to freeze hundreds of millions of rands' worth of Gupta assets in a bid to recover the money paid to Estina. Since then, the assets have been released and the NPA has 'provisionally' withdrawn charges against the Guptas, apparently due to lack of cooperation from authorities in India and the United Arab Emirates, where much of the siphoned money seems to have ended up. Meanwhile, the dairy farm at Vrede is in ruins and Ajay Gupta has confidently predicted that the case will never again see the light of day.

CHAPTER SIX

Space to graze:
cattle and the land question

'The land shall be shared among those who work it,' declares Section Four of South Africa's Freedom Charter, officially adopted by the Congress of the People in Kliptown, Soweto, in June 1955. The Charter continues:

> Restrictions of land ownership on a racial basis shall be ended, and all the land redivided ... Freedom of movement shall be guaranteed to all who work on the land; All shall have the right to occupy land wherever they choose; People shall not be robbed of their cattle ...

Forty-one years later, on 8 May 1996, this sentiment was cemented in the South African Constitution, which entitles those whose land tenure was rendered insecure due to past racially discriminatory laws either to tenure or to compensation, and allows for the state to carry out the compulsory expropriation of land in order to advance land reform and more equitable access to the country's natural resources. Prudently, the Constitution leaves the task of determining how land reform should be carried out, and what land reform should seek to achieve, to the legislative and executive arms of government.

Progress since then towards realising these fine commitments has been painfully slow. By early 2018, the South African government

– despite promises by the ANC to transfer 30% of the country's commercial farmland to black people by 2014 – had transferred only 9.54 million hectares, about 9% of the total.

By 2019, an election year, the so-called 'land question' was looming ever larger in South African politics, with the Economic Freedom Fighters (EFF) and many within the ruling party putting pressure on the ANC leadership to speed up land reform, including amending the very constitution that proposed it in the first place to allow for expropriation without compensation by the state. At the time of writing, a motion to amend the South African Constitution to this end had been endorsed by parliament, the country's main law-making body, and a parliamentary committee had been tasked with drafting the new constitutional clause.

You cannot farm cattle, or anything else for that matter, without land. Land – who has it, who does not but should have, and what the state's role in all this should be – is thus rightfully a burning topic in contemporary South Africa. Of late, President Ramaphosa has repeatedly emphasised that South Africa needs a land reform programme that addresses what he calls the country's 'original sin' but does so in ways that do not compromise food security or scare away investors. Beyond that, there is still little clarity as to what the future holds.

Amid all the debate about under what circumstances it is necessary to expropriate white-owned commercial farmland, not much has yet been said about the 10% of South African land that is state-owned, or the 15% that is still held communally. There are other fundamental questions that remain unanswered too, including whether land reform should aim primarily to produce a large number of subsistence farmers or a smaller number of black commercial farmers. Yet South Africa is not alone in grappling with these questions. Along with Zimbabwe, whose land reform efforts to date have attracted few fans, Namibia too has travelled down this path, and Namibia's experiences, both its successes and its failures, hold some interesting lessons for the country.

Postcards from Namibia

Namibia's commercial livestock farming sector is, anyway, intimately entwined with South Africa's. According to Harald Marggraff, the commodities manager at the Namibia Agriculture Union – whose email address is simply, nay heroically, 'meat@...' – livestock is Namibia's main commercial agricultural commodity, with weaners destined for South African feedlots featuring prominently:

> We don't have feedlots in Namibia because we don't produce enough maize. For every kilo of meat from a feedlot we would have to import seven kilos of maize. It wouldn't make sense. So instead we export our weaners to South Africa. Roughly half our weaners go this route. The other half are slaughtered here in Namibia. Exactly how it works out each year depends on the maize price. When the maize price is low, the feedlots in South Africa all want our cattle. When the maize price is high, they don't. Weaner prices drop and more cattle stay this side. It is a cycle but overall I'd say it's about 50/50.

Like South Africa, since gaining independence in 1990, Namibia has also had to deal with the question of how best to redistribute scarce agricultural land and overcome the multiple inequalities of the past. Unlike South Africa, however, Namibia has the Red Line: a veterinary cordon that runs across the north of the country from east to west, separating predominantly communal black farmers to the north from predominantly commercial white farmers in central and southern Namibia.

The Red Line was implemented by German colonists in 1896 in the hope of preventing the spread of rinderpest from the former Transvaal. It derives its name from the red ink that imperial cartographers used to demarcate the line on their maps. Even though the cordon completely failed to contain the virus – by 1897 rinderpest had crossed Namibia's eastern border and reached Windhoek before Dr Koch's vaccinations could contain the disease – the Red Line has endured. These days, its main purpose is to reassure international markets that cattle and beef from south of the line are free of foot-and-mouth disease and lung sickness. Farmers south of the line are permitted to export their produce across the world at premium prices, while farmers north of the line are restricted to selling their meat as decidedly unpremium 'factory' meats or LFTB – even if their animals are healthy and infection-free.

If above-the-line beef is exported at all, it is only to South Africa and other neighbouring countries like Angola and the Democratic Republic of the Congo. These restrictions depress incomes in the poor northern communal areas while making commercial agricultural development there even more difficult.

To find out how the Namibian government is negotiating the legacy of the Red Line, I travelled to Windhoek to meet with Gizaw Negussie, an Ethiopian senior technical advisor for the Meat Board of Namibia. According to Negussie, in 2007, the Namibian government and the country's commercial agricultural sector reached a compromise: the government would collect a voluntary levy from the beef and cattle exports of commercial farms south of the line and use the money to train farmers north of the line in commercial farming. The idea was that this would, at some point, give these farmers a chance to get into wider export markets.

About N$40 million was collected, and it was Negussie's job to administer the fund's mentorship programme. When asked how it was going, Negussie sighed quietly and looked up at the ceiling of his air-conditioned office:

We are reviewing the programme. We are finding that many of the farmers in the communal areas simply do not want to sell their cattle. They have few alternatives to invest their money. If you are near a bank, you could put the money from the cattle in the bank. But if there are no banks near, why would you do that?

Another challenge, Negussie said, was the availability of grazing in such a dry country:

> Where there is adequate grazing, our mentorship programme is yielding results. Cattle mortality rates are down, fertility is up. Calving rates climb. But where grazing is a limiting factor, you don't see much change.

Negussie reckoned there were around 800 000 cattle south of the Red Line and around 1.3 million north of it. He said that most of the cattle north of the line were mixed Nguni, while most of those south of it were larger, imported breeds. Whichever side of the line Namibians live, Negussie reckoned, they all want cattle:

> In this country, everyone from the watchmen to the prime minister have cattle. People think of Namibia as so empty, but there is a limit to how far this set-up is sustainable. We are, in fact, running out of space.

In 2015, two years after I met him, Negussie co-wrote an article claiming the mentorship programme had changed the perceptions of farmers in communal lands about commercial cattle farming. The article cited as evidence that, while it had initially been the programme's intention to train 350 farmers in commercial farming over a 12-month period, in the end 899 farmers were trained, and of these nearly half had subsequently started doing commercial farmer-like things, such as deworming their animals, while 39% had started giving their cattle food supplements.

Encouraging as all this sounded, the article carefully avoided any mention of whether any of the trainees had become viable commercial cattle farmers. With the Red Line in place – and showing no signs of being lifted following a severe outbreak of foot-and-mouth disease in 2015 – the chances seem small.

Of course, there are always exceptions. The day after meeting Negussie, I met Charles/Urib, a Damara cattle breeder who moved between his business in the capital and his 8 000-hectare farm 500 km away, north of the Red Line. /Urib said:

> I grew up on a farm and I always wanted one of my own. And now I do own one! At first I rented the land, but then I bought the farm in 2010. Without any government money. I started with just 50 cattle, but now I have 180 stud and around 500 commercial herd.

/Urib started farming Ngunis but soon became dissatisfied with their low body weight, instead switching to Simbras – a cross between Swiss Simmental and American Brahman cattle – for his stud-farming operation. /Urib regularly auctions off cattle from his commercial herd, usually to either Meatco or to South African feedlots:

> I breed bulls and sell them on stud auctions. They are very fertile, very adapted, and their weaners have higher kilos than other cattle.

Despite the auctions, /Urib confessed that the farm wasn't exactly profitable:

> To tell you the truth, I make my money at my business in Windhoek and spend it on the farm. The farm does generate an income, but not yet a profit. But at some stage that will come. I hope it will be in my generation. So far I have three daughters, but no sons. So I don't know what will happen in the future.

To prove that he is serious about making a commercial success of his farm, /Urib joined the Namibia Agriculture Union, the country's oldest farmers' union, rather than the Namibia National Farmers Union, which focuses on both commercial and emerging farmers:

> I know the Namibia Agriculture Union is mostly white farmers, but I don't care. Things are not like before. I am optimistic. Very optimistic. I have a lot of plans.

One of /Urib's major accomplishments, he reckoned, was securing a loan from the state-owned Agribank of Namibia, which was founded in 1907 under the moniker *Deutsch-Südwestafrikanischer Farmerbund* to promote agriculture by providing financing to farmers.

It is pretty hard to get credit as a farmer. It is very hard to get loans from Agribank. I don't know why. Maybe it is because I am not politically connected. But anyway, I have finally got a loan … it was third time lucky. The interest rate is much lower than commercial loans.

In addition to providing finance, Agribank runs the Farmers' Support Project, a joint initiative co-funded by the German development agency, GIZ, which aims to prepare emerging farmers for commercial farming. One of the programme's mentors, Leon Burger, has a farm near Tsumeb, in the Oshikoto region just south of the Red Line, where he keeps goats and 500 cattle. In addition to running his own farm, Burger works with farmers in the communal lands across the Red Line:

Yes, it is a lot to be doing, but I always say that if you are a commercial farmer and you say there's too much work, and you've no time for anything else, then you are doing it wrong.

Wise words, I thought, about … well … almost anything. Mentoring, Burger said, was harder than it looked:

Our farmers north of the Red Line, they see their cattle numbers as their wealth. But from my perspective, the land there is totally overstocked. As a mentor on commercial farming, you have to convince them to sell. I have been trying, but it is not easy. It is just not their traditional way. They only want to sell when the cattle are old, and so the price is low. But some are listening to what we mentors are saying. Especially when you bring in ways to increase their calving rates, with licks and animal health products.

Perhaps, then, the Red Line is not the greatest obstacle to the commercial success for farmers on communal lands in the north. Perhaps a greater challenge is that of diverging world views: of African farmers wanting their cattle alive and white commercial beef farmers urging them to cash in on their cattle's hastened deaths.

A dystopian vision of land taxation and redistribution

A few years after achieving independence in 1990, the Namibian government implemented a land tax to fund its land reform effort. Not surprisingly, the tax has been unpopular with the commercial farmers being taxed. Harry Schneider-Waterberg, the owner of a guest lodge and a vast, 40 000-hectare cattle farm near the Waterberg plateau outside Otjiwarongo, north of Windhoek, was particularly impassioned in his denunciation of the tax when I spoke to him:

> Why should we pay? I know. I have a huge farm, even by Namibian standards. But look at the bigger picture. Ten percent of land in this country belongs to the state. Forty-five percent is communal. That leaves 45% commercial. Now already 35% of commercial land has gone to black people. That is a big success. We are well over half way to our target. Must we speed it up when we know that the more farms are redistributed, the less the commercial sector produces?

Guessing what I might be thinking, Schneider-Waterberg added quickly:

> That's not racism. It took me ten years to get this farm producing. And that is without my having to buy it first. And it has taken two generations of commercial farming knowledge. And a university degree and blah blah blah. With the resettlement farms, they don't have the commercial farming knowledge or the capital. And whose farm is it really? Is it theirs or the government's? That's a question. So of course things fall back towards subsistence farming.

In addition to the land tax, the independent Namibian government started buying farms from white commercial farmers south of the Red Line, subdividing the land and parcelling out plots to black Namibian applicants who were able to prove that they have at least 150 cattle.

This was not the best approach, according to Willem 'Hennie' Brisley, another mentor with the Farmers' Support Project:

> [The government] has been subdividing 5 000-hectare farms into four, but that can't work. It is not enough land. Not in Namibia. Our land is too harsh … there is livestock overstocking, and before you know it, the land deteriorates and ends up looking like the communal lands. Calving rates go down and the government gets embarrassed, but they carry on giving out land this way. I think the people who are getting the land are politically connected. It must be. The ship is sinking, but at least we are trying to mend the holes.

Brisley, who holds an animal science degree from the University of Pretoria, invited me along on a trip to one of his projects, Aruvlei, an 8 000-hectare farm, formerly owned by one farmer, now home to 150 households.

Aruvlei is south of Windhoek, well away from the Red Line in the country's central Khomas region. We drove out early one morning in Brisley's bakkie, past spectacular mountain ranges that looked like they could go on forever until, suddenly, we turned left off the road and there was the farm.

Aruvlei was, as Brisley had warned, in a bedraggled state. Vehicles and equipment lay around in varying stages of disrepair. Most residents' homes were in need of loving attention. Despite the poor condition of the farm, Brisley loved mentoring there. The people he worked with were eager to learn, and mentoring had taught him a lot, forcing him to re-evaluate much of what he thought he knew about commercial agriculture and decision-making:

> I have learned that at Aruvlei, the problem is not just what I first thought it was, about animal health and husbandry among emerging farmers – although that is a real issue. We found that

the neighbouring commercial farmers, white farmers, were buying up the livestock of these guys for too cheap. So now we have got these resettlement farmers in an association, so they can negotiate their prices better. In all this, I've been learning from these farmers too about how to decide things together. When something needs deciding, these guys decide it. But in my townhouse complex in Windhoek we have been arguing for three months about the colour we are going to repaint it.

This sentiment was echoed by Elaine Smith, senior manager of the Farmers' Support Project. When asked whether the project was working, she gave a slight laugh and said:

The expectations around this project are huge, huge, and everyone asks that question. One project benchmark is whether more cattle are being sold for slaughter from farmers north of the Red Line. Another is whether there is a rise in these farmers' incomes. But the project is about much more than that. It is about where we are in Namibia, about cultural issues. It is about how to give advice, and how to receive advice. In the end, it is about good neighbourly relations between commercial and communal farmers in this country.

Back on Aruvlei, Brisley drove his bakkie from homestead to homestead, soon busying himself with deworming goats. We eventually came to Ernestine, whose goats were in finer fettle than most. Ernestine also had nine mixed-breed cattle with strong Brahman traits, which she kept mainly for milk. Unlike many of her neighbours, she regarded herself as a career farmer:

I have been 13 years on this farm. My grandmother was here. Then it was my aunt. Now it is me. Many people on this farm stay in town and just come at weekends, but not me. I am here every day. I am serious about farming. Not everyone here is serious about farming like me. [But] grazing is hard. We are waiting for the rain. But I have bought supplements for my cattle with my own money.

When asked if she ever sold her goats and cattle, Ernestine said:

If I have 150 goats, then I will start to sell. With my cattle I will sell if my herd goes over 20. I must have at least 15 cattle. Nine is not many. I once had 25 cattle. Yes. But I sold them. I sold them to a lady in Windhoek. She has a small butchery there.

Later, Brisley told me that Ernestine was among the most dynamic and productive farmers on Aruvlei:

The pace of the other guys frustrates Ernestine. I think she wants to move to another farm. I don't know how that will go, but if Ernestine ever does, it will be good for her. But I really wonder what will happen to Aruvlei.

Freddie Hertzberg, a livestock trader from Otjimbingwe, was no fan of resettlement farms either. As we drove down a succession of dirt tracks towards a resettlement farm, he regaled me with his views:

Look! It is such a mess! Look at all the rubbish everywhere! There are seven families on this particular farm. With five of them, [they were awarded the land] because a member of the family was in the army or police. And they are all Oshivambo [the German term for Ovambo people]! This was never traditionally their land, and here they are destroying it with overgrazing.

There are then, evidently, no easy solutions to the land-use challenges Namibia continues to confront, but South Africa can still learn from its northern neighbour's experience. For one, it is seriously hard to turn a profit as a first-generation commercial farmer. Those giving it a try need to have access to inexpensive and sufficient credit to stand a better chance of pulling through. A second lesson is that transferring commercial farms to multiple new owners presents multiple unanticipated challenges, including, as we saw, considerable divergence in the farming skills of the new arrivals, leaving the best farmers among the new owners frustrated by their less motivated peers. It also emerges that improving emerging farmers' negotiating position vis-à-vis their commercial farmer neighbours is an important but largely overlooked part of the land reform process. Finally, and this theme comes up time and again in this book, Namibia's experience shows us that advice and mentorship by commercial farmers does not in itself shift the deep-rooted preference that sits in so many emerging farmers for their cattle to remain alive and with them, and not sold off for profit and slaughter.

The land back home

Back home, there has been a long-running lack of clarity in the South African government's vision about what it wants from land reform. Does it intend that land reform should uplift the poorest of the poor, or that it should rather mainly help emerging black farmers transition to commercial farming? Should farms be awarded primarily to communities for them to farm en masse, or should it be given to fewer individuals in the hope that these beneficiaries become a new elite of black commercial farmers? And what role should the government, white commercial farmers and financial institutions play in this transition?

Looking, if not for answers, then at least for insights, I travelled one winter to the beautiful Carnarvon Estate – an old, large livestock farm in the foothills of the snow-capped Stormberg mountains, 50 km from Queenstown in the Eastern Cape.

The emerging black commercial farmer

Carnarvon Estate is owned by the president of the National Emerging Red Meat Producers Organisation, Aggrey Mahanjana. The state purchased the land from the Halse family, which had owned it since 1854, and gave it to Mahanjana in 2009 as part of its land reform programme. Frederick Halse, the farm's first owner, was the third son of Cornishman Thomas Halse, who was one of the 1820 settlers. Mahanjana's own father had been a maize and livestock farmer on communal lands, while his mother taught in farm schools around Bathurst and Port Alfred.

> When I was young, I would travel around with my mother. I would see these white farmers, like Mr Green. Mr Green seemed so rich. My dream was to be like him. I didn't know then that it was all based on loans from the bank.

Mahanjana studied agriculture at Fort Hare and then Pretoria University, in the process becoming one of South Africa's few vocal black agricultural policy theorists and advocates. He was delighted when the Eastern Cape Department of Land Affairs awarded him Carnarvon, but after a few years on the property, he conceded that actually working the land was very different to studying farming:

> I learned all the theory in college but here, on the land, you must plan according to the reality of your particular farm.

When I visited him, Mahanjana kept about 1 000 sheep and about 300 head of cattle – 50 shorthorn, 50 Ngunis (although he had recently deregistered the herd) and a mixed herd of about 200. He sold weaners to feedlots at between seven and nine months, which explained his aversion to Ngunis, which are lean in build and don't fatten up easily. But his main source of income was selling water to the local municipality:

> I have learned that there is no money in farming as a first-generation farmer. Whatever you have is because of your loans. It is only in the third and fourth generations that you see the guys making money, unless they are given things for free by the government. All I was given was the lease.

I asked if Mahanjana's children were interested in farming. He laughed. His son, he said, wanted to do music and film. So was it all worth it?

He nodded his head:

> Look. In the past, I had a dream. Today, I have achieved the reality behind my dream. It is not the same as the dream, but it is reality. That is what liberation has been to me: a chance to live in reality, not dreams.

We turned to the subject of land reform. Mahanjana believed that farms transferred from white to black hands should remain commercially viable. Too often, he said, farms were given to people with no money to run them:

> A farm is like a crocodile … it wants to be fed. So many people have been given farms but, because they have no money, they sell their produce just for their consumption needs. So there is no investment, and the farm goes down.

To ensure the success of land reform, Mahanjana argued, South Africa's black farmers needed access to sufficient, affordable credit, just as Afrikaner farmers received during the apartheid era. In Mahanjana's ideal world, the Land Bank would provide interest-free start-up loans to emerging farmers so that they could buy farm machinery and livestock; farmers' co-operatives would lend to farmers at minimal interest rates; and commercial banks (with their commercial interest rates) would be a last resort. The reality was the opposite: with credit from the Land Bank and farmers' co-operatives largely unavailable, allegedly due to woeful underfunding, most black farmers are forced to choose between commercial bank loans or no credit at all.

Mahanjana was deeply critical of the Eastern Cape Department of Agriculture's lack of capacity and direction, and the national government's lack of clarity on whether it wanted to see black subsistence or black commercial farmers:

> Our politicians … they might want many cattle for themselves, but they are not really commercial farmers. They come from the

townships. That is a big change from the past. In the previous white government, half the Cabinet were commercial farmers. They understood its challenges.

For all the difficulties, Mahanjana remains strongly in favour of land redistribution, saying it is a must if South Africa is to survive. He believes that, to redistribute enough land, the state should have the right of first refusal on all land sales. However, land should only be redistributed to black farmers who could make a go of it.

To achieve this, Mahanjana proposed, land should initially be leased to new recipients for three to five years, to test whether they meet the required standards and so mitigate the risks. He didn't explain how emerging farmers would be able to access affordable credit if they were only leasing their land and could well lose it, although he did suggest pooling expensive farming equipment to broaden access to it for cash-strapped black farmers.

Mahanjana was vehemently opposed to land expropriation without compensation. It took no account of the money land owners had spent on improving the land, he argued, and would discourage investment in agriculture. He also said that a great deal of land in communal areas now lay fallow because farmers no longer had access to the labour needed to work it. The state should turn this land, he said, into commercial farms.

> When I was young, we never hired farming labour. Even if there were no children to do it, we never paid for help in cash. Instead, you would give a calf, a sack of maize. But these days it's money or nothing. All the children have gone and our farmers in the communal areas do not have the money to hire.

Mahanjana conceded that white-owned commercial farmland was usually in better condition than communal land, but said better-quality land typically came with higher costs, too. It was the same as driving a car, he said:

You don't start with a Mercedes-Benz. You start with a smaller car. One that's cheaper to run and easier to fix.

The farming politician

A few years after I met Mahanjana, I was invited to the farm of Zweli Mkhize, a former premier of KwaZulu-Natal and ANC treasurer who was appointed Minister of Health in 2019. Mkhize's farm is a beautiful, long stretch of thornveld not far from Pietermaritzburg, with tree-lined, undulating hills nearby and cliff-faced higher peaks out in the distance, their rocks turning golden pink as the day wears on.

The farm is mostly given over to sugarcane, though Mkhize also keeps an Nguni herd. Mkhize said he comes to the farm whenever he can:

The farm takes my focus away from politics. It completely distracts me.

Whenever Mkhize visits, he always spends time with his cattle, watching them closely:

You must look at how they walk. There must be no limping and no stiffness. And you must feel their temperatures. There is so much game around here that the ticks carry a lot of diseases, hard water, red water, gall sickness. These can decimate your herd. Herefords, Frieslands and Jerseys won't last long here. But Ngunis can cope.

Mkhize pointed to a cow that was looking at us:

Look at this one. She is standing still. She has lifted her head. And look at her ears. She is observing us. She is listening to us. She is inspecting us. It is because she has a calf nearby that she is nursing. That is all fine. If her ears were drooping, I would be worried. That would mean she is sick.

Mkhize grew up with cattle on a farm not far from Imbali, a township of Pietermaritzburg, where his father was a farm labourer. Mkhize was only three years old when he started herding cattle. They formed an important link between him and his father.

> My father passed when I was eight years old. He was a disciplinarian. 'Where are the cattle?' he would ask me. 'Why are they not all in?' That kind of thing. I remember, there were five cattle born when he was very sick and had gone to stay at an inyanga's. The cattle had lovely hides. I had given them names. I wanted to tell my father the names but he never came back home.

The white farmer who owned the land demanded that each Mkhize boy work on his farm between the ages of 13 and 14, completely disrupting their education. When it was Mkhize's turn, the family defied the farmer and, to his ire, flatly refused to give him up. The family was allowed to stay on the farm for a while, but soon after, the farmer sold up and they were all evicted. For Mkhize's part, he went on to finish his studies and become a medical doctor.

Mkhize knows his history and is well versed in Zulu culture. He loves the use of elegant bovine metaphor in everyday speech and the naming of cattle:

> In English, you would say looks are deceiving. But in Zulu we talk of ukumisa. Ukumisa is the shape of a cow's horns, and we have a phrase that means you cannot judge the strength of a cow from the shape of its horns.
>
> With Ngunis, no one hide is quite like another. So we have become very creative in describing them. That one is brown with a lot of white sprinkled ... have you ever had wheat bread and put amasi with it, the amasi with sorghum granules? It is a colour like that. We say imvubomabele.

Such descriptions were employed, said Mkhize, during lobola negotiations, when the groom's representatives would wax lyrical about the cattle they intended to pay in discussions with the bride's team, according to a carefully considered sequence:

It is poetic in the way it is performed. In the olden days, people would remember the order the cattle were first presented so when you came by a year later, they would tell you about each one in the same order. They remembered the colours.

Despite his love of Zulu culture and the role cattle play in it, Mkhize does not believe in keeping herds of cattle 'for their own sake'.

I have given some of the cattle from this herd for lobola payments from my family, but that is not why I keep this herd. This is a commercial herd, and the idea is to sell cattle, mainly bull yearlings, to other breeders.

Mkhize also advocated the classic commercial farmer's approach of keeping numbers down to 'sustainable levels' and rotating the herd through continuous sales and purchases.

What worked back in the past for our community, when the tradition formed, does not necessarily suit today's times. We know that our people still have so much attachment to their cattle, but you don't get revenue from these animals and at the same time each one of these cattle needs four hectares. Do our people have that land?

Mkhize shook his head, paused briefly, then continued:

But with half a hectare, you can put in poultry, you can have thousands of birds that you can sell every week. People must realise that these days you cannot have large herds of cattle, like we did in the past. We have smaller spaces now, and we have no choice. We have to adapt.

When it came to economic upliftment through agriculture, Mkhize said the government needed to improve access to the market for black subsistence farmers who want to become commercial farmers:

> Right now, the market is not working for subsistence farmers. The market is too advanced for these farmers and they cannot access it. This is a huge task for us in government. It means training at every level: to get the volumes, with processing, with marketing. We want regional processing hubs that can create sustainable livelihoods. If we could do this, we would finally make a dent in rural unemployment.

It was refreshing to hear a senior politician from the ruling party who sounded clear-headed about what he thought was needed to make land reform work. Still, I could not help but wonder if this implied that Mkhize thought the government's efforts to transform agriculture and redistribute land had failed. Mkhize denied this, saying that while land reform might not have worked particularly well economically thus far, the programme was working politically, by reassuring people that change was happening and thus buying the ANC time to implement a controlled process of transformation:

> It is land reform from this government that has given the country stability. If we had not been able to create a space for our people to feel the new dispensation was beginning to open up – both in terms of land ownership and business opportunities – you would have people just invading the farms and taking them over. In fact, the protests we are seeing all over the country are the ones that we allayed 20 years ago with land reform and the restitution process.

Neatly sidestepping the question of whether the government's land reform programme had done enough in those 20 years, Mhkize conceded that the problem now faced was ensuring that land reform was 'sustainable'. Sustainable, Mkhize said, meant ensuring that commercial farmland transferred to black people remains capable of producing a marketable surplus, and does not revert to subsistence.

However, he added softly:

There has been a lot of weakness on that one.

Academic viewpoints

The idea that communal farmers need to become commercial farmers if land reform is to be a success is overly simplistic, according to Professor Ben Cousins of the Institute for Poverty, Land and Agrarian Studies (PLAAS) at the University of the Western Cape. There is, Cousins told me, a neglected middle way small-scale production.

Small-scale farming is seen by many people as a vestige of the past. There is a disregard for small-scale production, and consequently there is neglect of it from government.

PLAAS is arguably the country's premier academic department for research on both land reform and food production. A consistent hallmark of PLAAS's work is that its analysis is always firmly grounded in context, taking due account of the country's deep historic and structural inequalities.

Cousins believes that new forms of land ownership need to be explored, forms that fall somewhere between communal and commercial single-owner – the agricultural equivalent, if you will, of sectional title in a block of flats. This was not the same thing, explained Cousins, as resettling a large number of people all belonging to a single trust on a commercial farm, which, as we saw earlier in the chapter in relation to Namibia, does not often work out well. It is more likely to mean settling a commercial farm with a smaller number of emerging farmers and delineating carefully which farm assets are communally owned and for which there is communal responsibility, and which assets now belong to the farmers individually. That kind of reasoning, I thought, should appeal to an ANC government, but according to Cousins, so far it has not:

There have been rhetorical flourishes from the government in this direction, but little actual subdivision of land. They are frightened that it will make the land unproductive.

In marked contrast to Mahanjana's tale of governmental neglect, Cousins contended that the ANC is far *too* focused on helping black commercial farmers, which he described as a classic case of 'elite capture'. He also dismissed as disingenuous Mkhize's argument that land reform was being progressively realised over time. Instead, Cousins alleged, innovative thinking about land nosedived when Thoko Didiza, when she was the Minister of Agriculture and Land Affairs between 1999 and 2006, reversed the government's policy on area-based planning, a progressive concept that integrates land and agrarian reform, and rooted out of her department both older white employees and progressive land-reform academics and activists who had come in since 1994:

It was tragic. All the learning was lost.

Gugile Nkwinti, Didiza's successor in the position of Minister of Rural Development and Land Reform until 2018, when President Cyril Ramaphosa replaced him, was often hailed as one of the brighter stars in Zuma's dimly lit Cabinet. But, in Cousins' view, he was little different:

Nkwinti spoke radical rhetoric, but in practice he supported the chiefs and the commercial farmers. And on the ground, under his watch, the department rapidly fell apart.

According to Cousins, the earlier area-based planning policy was resurrected by the Department of Land Affairs under Nkwinti, but there had been such a hollowing-out of capacity in both the local and national administration by then that its implementation was mostly farmed out to consultants, most of whom, Cousins said, used 'a cut and paste approach' rather than digging more deeply, and had achieved little impact.

I asked Cousins where the national Ministry of Agriculture, Forestry and Fisheries was in all this. The unfortunate answer, he replied, was nowhere at all. Since 1994, successive national Ministers of Agriculture have pledged to harmonise the state's agricultural and land reform policies. However, provincial departments of agriculture – over which white commercial farmers still have considerable influence – have done precious little to translate that aspiration into reality. Additionally, state-funded agricultural extension services have largely withered since 1994, hitting emerging black commercial farmers, who are unable to seek private support, the hardest.

The bottom line, said Cousins, is that land reform will always be a 'win-lose' situation: no matter how you spin it, resources will always need to be transferred from one party to another. It requires a capable state and strong political will to achieve this, and Cousins' view, speaking as he was before Zuma's fall from power, was that South Africa had neither.

Were the opposition parties any better? Cousins was sceptical:

> The DA is wedded to the free market, to the commercial farming model. The EFF talks so unrealistically about land … The ANC doesn't know what it wants. AgriSA are interesting, though. They need to be seen to be doing things. With political will, they could actually do something.

AgriSA, founded in 1904 as the South African Agricultural Union and today consisting of nine provincial unions and 24 commodity organisations, is the country's oldest commercial farming association. It is not an institution usually associated with anything close to progressive thinking. Yet, if white South African commercial farmers have learnt anything from their Zimbabwean counterparts, it is the importance of being proactive in ensuring that land reform takes place in ways they can more or less live with. Failing to do so risks a government down the line imposing another version that sees them having to pack their bags.

Appointing his new cabinet in 2019, Ramaphosa showed signs that he was listening to critiques of the government's efforts on land reform, merging the ministries of agriculture, rural development and land reform and thus paving the way – perhaps – for more policy co-ordination. Yet the president's choice of minister, Didiza, whom Cousins has credited with doing such damage to the cause of land reform, is likely to leave many disappointed. Meanwhile, Ramaphosa's Expert Advisory Panel on Land Reform submitted its report in June 2019. That the panel initially included the president of AgriSA is an indication of the association's profile in the agricultural sector and the government's willingness to listen to alternative views. How the panel has reached consensus on a way forward for the country remains to be seen. Ominously, AgriSA's president and 'at least one other member' have refused to sign the panel's report because of conflict around land expropriation without compensation. The Presidency responded by issuing a statement pointing out that capturing conflicting views was exactly what the panel had been asked to do.

Also appointed to the Expert Advisory Panel on Land Reform was Professor Mohammad Karaan, the Dean of the Faculty of AgriSciences at the University of Stellenbosch, whom I had sought out several years earlier to learn more about the challenges of agricultural reform.

Seated comfortably behind his desk in a large office at the university, looking out onto a leafy, prosperous Stellenbosch street, Karaan told me that he was Indian-Malay by birth, and that his maternal grandfather had been a farmer in the old Transkei before the apartheid government decreed that Indians could no longer own land in the bantustans. When Karaan enrolled at the university in 1987, he was the only black student in the AgriSciences faculty. He graduated in 1992, returning four years later to join the teaching staff. Today, he is the department's first non-white dean.

Karaan served on the board of the Land Bank until his resignation in August 2017. He was also part of the National Planning Commission that wrote South Africa's National Development Plan (NDP), which steers government policy but was largely ignored by Zuma's scandal-distracted administration. Under Ramaphosa, prospects for the NDP's implementation seem brighter. On the land question, and in line with the Constitution as originally drafted, the NDP advocates compulsory land expropriation by the state, but with compensation. It calls for more farmland to be transferred from white to black hands, recommending that part of the state's land purchases be funded by those white farmers who are permitted to retain their properties.

Karaan believed established white farmers should be tasked with mentoring new black commercial farmers, along the lines of Namibia's land reform programme. He, too, was concerned about farmers' access to credit:

> Black commercial farmers that I come across mostly have the wrong type of debt. Their debt should be interest-free, or at least low interest, and it should be spread over 40 years. That's what you need to establish a farm. But the best most of them can get is 20 years at commercial rates.

Despite funding challenges, Karaan expected the number of black commercial farmers to increase, filling a vacuum created by white farmers abandoning their land because farming would increasingly fail to generate the high returns on investment that they have grown accustomed to. New black entrants to the sector, Karaan reasoned, would have more modest expectations. The challenge for these new farmers, however, would be a shortage of affordable financial and intellectual capital:

> Of course black farmers are intelligent enough to farm, but intellectual capital is a different thing. In farming, you need that intellectual capital, the networks, the knowledge and experience going back generations ... White farmers were often born on farms run by their parents, went to agricultural school, then to

agricultural college, and then to work on someone else's farm before trying it themselves. Fifty percent of the Afrikaners at this faculty have farming connections. You don't see that with black farmers. I fear that few of them will make it.

Karaan seemed momentarily saddened by this conclusion, but then his tone suddenly brightened:

Things are going wrong now, yes, but we have the opportunity to fix them. South Africa, in its diversity, is a test tube of God's creation. And God did not create all this to fail. If the right leader comes, the country has a great future.

The optimism was heartening though not entirely convincing, particularly for those who do not share Karaan's view that South Africa is a divine showcase for successful diversity in action and, therefore, simply too blessed to fail.

Required reading for the Expert Panel as it deliberates was, one hopes, *Cattle Ownership and Production in the Communal Areas of the Eastern Cape, South Africa*, a 2002 research report by PLAAS, edited by academic Andrew Ainslie, who was also the lead author.

In his contribution to the report, and as we saw also in Namibia, Ainslie argues that successive South African governments have failed to convince farmers in communal areas to embrace commercial farming values because they have never done the hard work of trying to understand why communal farmers continue to resist this change of mindset. Not helping the authorities in their planning is that livestock in communal areas has persistently been undercounted, in part because it has been assumed by official statisticians that only livestock reared for the commercial beef market and slaughtered in abattoirs even *counts* as livestock production.

More importantly, Ainslie also reiterated a point that cropped up again and again in my interviews: farmers in communal areas do not keep cattle only for their beef. They want their cattle alive, to provide draught power, milk, prestige, joy, lobola and an ancestral connection. Indeed, communal farmers attach a higher value to these cattle precisely because of their non-beef and non-market uses.

In a powerful critique of schemes like the farm mentoring programme in Namibia and the Industrial Development Corporation's (IDC's) Nguni programme in South Africa (discussed in the next chapter), Ainslie concluded:

> The notion that a small group of full-time, 'committed' commercial farmers exist 'out there' that might be identified … is one that has spawned a number of previous studies, launched multi-million-rand irrigation schemes and 'farmer support schemes', and still tantalises some analysts and policy makers. However, given the political and economic realities that exist, the establishment of a 'yeoman class' of any depth remains an illusion.

Instead, Ainslie advocated 'more nuanced, historically informed perspectives' that embrace 'actor-directed change' rather than change due to outside intervention by experts, to be imposed on the obdurate peasantry once all the necessary 'consultation' boxes have been ticked. Politicians would do well to heed Ainslie's counsel, or else risk wasting scarce public funds on yet more ill-conceived and unwanted initiatives that, even if they are not fleeced by corrupt officials, still end up under- or unused because the people they are intended to benefit have other ideas.

Delving deeper into this love of cattle, in the next chapter we look at South Africa's famous indigenous breed, the Nguni. Once written off as scrawny and unproductive 'kaffir cattle', Nguni are now seen in a new light, lauded for their beauty, climate crisis adaptability, and for their apparent capacity to help effect both economic and environmental transformation.

CHAPTER SEVEN

Ngunis and new cow economics

The Nguni is the darling breed of indigenous South African cattle. Once derided by white farmers as genetically inferior to European cattle, Ngunis are intelligent, sociable, fertile and increasingly appreciated for their hardiness and beautiful hides.

Unlike most European breeds, Nguni cattle have not been bred to produce lots of milk or have a large rump. African livestock farmers are usually prepared to accept whatever progeny their cattle deliver without trying to influence the result. Indeed, the Zulu people I met in northern KwaZulu-Natal told me they saw in the details of new calves – the shape of their horns and the colour of their hides in particular – communications from the family ancestors. The result of all these many years of non-breeding is that today's Nguni cattle are well-balanced, adaptable all-rounders that produce modest amounts of milk and modest amounts of meat. Despite being more drought-resistant, this makes them a poor fit for the mainstream commercial livestock sector, which remains hooked on supersized, imported breeds.

The king who loved Nguni cattle

Eswatini's late king, Sobhuza II, was known for his love for Nguni cattle; and it was he who initiated a process that would eventually lead to the South African Stud Book Society officially recognising the breed.

It all started the day King Sobhuza II asked Tim and Liz Reilly – who had helped establish the country's celebrated national parks, starting in 1964 with their own family farm, Mlilwane – 'Where are the native cattle?' Liz vividly recalled the day:

> We looked at him. We had no idea. But he was determined. He wanted to know what had happened to the cattle, which he said had once been everywhere but were now scarce.

Sobhuza assigned several members of his court to help the Reillys tour the country to identify Nguni cattle. Before long, Tim and Liz had found and purchased 20 Nguni cattle. Liz recalled:

> It started as a curiosity for us, I suppose. But the more we watched these cattle, the more we liked them. We saw they were much more capable of fending for themselves than our Simmentalers were. And they were wonderful aesthetically. So we showed them to the so-called livestock experts, and they said they were just 'kaffir beeste'.

Undeterred by the experts' response – or more probably spurred on – the Reillys set about acquiring a much larger Nguni herd, buying cattle from Swazi farmers for cash at dipping stations, or trading them for mixed-breed cattle from their own herd:

> We offered farmers two of our cattle for one of theirs. That was a good deal and helped persuade them to part with their beloved animals. But for us, it was an expensive exercise.

In 1981, the Reillys formally applied to the South African Stud Book Society to have Nguni cattle recognised as a breed. Even though the association already recognised several local cattle breeds, the application was only approved in 1983. Three years after that, the Nguni Cattle Breeders' Society was born, with the Reillys as founding members.

No improving on perfection

The Nguni Cattle Breeders' Society, which is still active today, strives to preserve the Nguni as a breed in the face of a commerce-driven push to 'improve' it, mostly by beefing it up. Most feedlots, traders and butchers dislike purebred Ngunis because they are lean and yield relatively little meat per carcass, even on a feedlot diet of hominy chop and supplements.

Lovers of Nguni cattle in their natural state regard this kind of over-feeding and supplementation as anathema. For them, the joy of the Nguni is in its hardiness and cost-efficiency. As one Nguni cattle farmer I met in the Swazi bushveld said:

> I have around 100 head in my herd. My Ngunis are simple to keep, they don't get heart-water disease and they don't cost much to look after. We dip them as little as possible to help build up their immunity, and they mostly look after themselves. The only thing is you have to mix it up a bit genetically.

The farmer had no time for South African cattle farmers across the border who insist on trying to improve on the nature of Ngunis:

> Those guys have forgotten what it is all about! They are spoiling their Nguni. They just can't help themselves from feeding the cattle extra, but they shouldn't. The cattle should be going out and looking for food for themselves. I agree that for that you need good veld. But if you raise your cattle like that, the milk will be delicious, and so will the beef.

Another way to bulk up cattle is to cross Ngunis with other breeds. Some South African farmers do just that: at the massive ZZ2 farm in Mooketsi, Limpopo province, the Van Zyl family breed PinZ^{2}yl cattle – a cross of Nguni and Pinzgauer cattle from the Pinzgau region of Salzburg, Austria. A farm manager at ZZ2, which is also the biggest tomato grower in the country, assured me that the PinZ^{2}yl preserves 'all the best' Nguni traits while inheriting the much bigger frame of the Pinzgauer. That a breeding programme focused on just one outcome – building body size – might upset delicate balances that have emerged by natural selection over millennia will probably surprise no-one but commercial livestock breeders, who characteristically retain a neo-Trumpian self-confidence that they can always do it better, and it remains to be seen whether the PinZ²yl, which was registered as a new cattle breed 'under evaluation' in 2009, is truly as hardy as a purebred Nguni.

Ngunis at the heart of social development

In 2004, the IDC launched an innovative programme intended to preserve the Nguni as a breed and, ambitiously, promote social upliftment in rural areas.

The IDC was established in 1940 to develop South Africa's domestic industrial capacity after World War II disrupted trade from Europe. During the National Party era, the IDC focused on petrochemicals and mining. Even though it diversified its focus after 1994, investing in Nguni cattle is still quite a stretch for the IDC, one that came about only because of the persistence of one man: Tommy Mohajane.

Mohajane, now in his sixties, was born in Alexandra, Johannesburg. He fled to Tanzania in his teens, an exile from the apartheid regime, before going on to obtain a doctorate in the United Kingdom. After 1994, Mohajane returned to South Africa – eager, as he put it, to make a difference. He soon found work at the IDC, where he focused on social upliftment in rural areas:

> Rural communities are always last in the queue when it comes to development, and in South Africa the issue is complicated by the legacy of bantustans. The grandparents are sitting there with the grandchildren. The parents are away in urban areas. Nine-tenths don't send a penny and go once a year with groceries. What to do?

Mohajane's answer: start a programme that lends Nguni cattle to rural applicants for five years, after which they must repay the same number they were given. Such is the fertility of Ngunis that five years is regarded as being long enough to leave behind the makings of a herd. To qualify, applicants needed to prove that they had land and water – and commit to keeping their herds pure.

The programme was piloted in in the Eastern Cape in 2004. By 2012, it had been rolled out to all the provinces except the Western Cape and KwaZulu-Natal. Each active province has a board of trustees – consisting of two people each from the IDC, the provincial government and a participating university – that is responsible for selecting beneficiaries. Until 2015, when he was compelled to retire, Mohajane sat on these boards. Even now, he keeps a watchful eye on proceedings.

The North West and Limpopo have benefited the most from the programme, receiving by 2018 6 000 Nguni cattle between about 1 750 farmers – about half the national total of 3 500 farmers – some of whom work together in co-operatives.

Mohajane believed the Nguni programme would economically uplift and restore the dignity of its beneficiaries. In this, he was correct: many have already returned cattle to the provincial trusts and today run profitable businesses with their herds. One Limpopo family that received cattle was even able to pay the university registration fees of their son after selling one cow. 'This project has enabled elderly people to restore their self-worth,' said Mohajane. 'The recipients of the cattle no longer rely on handouts from their children in urban areas that never come.'

Despite these successes, the Nguni programme has not been without controversy. In KwaZulu-Natal, the IDC started giving out cattle as part of the programme but soon stopped due to political uncertainty (the province has had three ministers of agriculture since 2013) and allegations of political interference. Contrary to Mohajane's original vision, some of the beneficiaries of the Nguni programme in the province were politically connected town dwellers, including a magistrate who received over 30 Ngunis but only sees them when he travels from his home in Vryheid to visit them on Sundays.

Other beneficiaries in KwaZulu-Natal were, however, real farmers – like the Mbheles, who own a farm of hilly, open grassland near the small town of Dundee in the north of the province. The Mbhele family used to farm in the Free State but left for KwaZulu-Natal because, Godfrey Mbhele said, they could not cope with the rampant stock theft. The Mbheles received 30 Ngunis through the IDC programme, and Mbhele said they would soon have to give back half that number. He said he loved his Ngunis but admitted that his family were struggling with the long-term nature of the only available business model:

> You will never get much for Ngunis from the feedlots, unless you crossbreed them first with heavier breeds. But this programme forbids that. You have to keep the Nguni pure, which means you can only profitably sell them as stud, and for their hides. And that takes time.

The Nguni programme had helped the Mbheles transition from subsistence to commercial farming, but at a cost. To keep his herd pure, Mbhele needed good fencing to separate the Nguni from the rest of his herd and the wandering cattle of his neighbours. The fencing was expensive and often stolen, and Mbhele hinted that once he had paid back the required number of cattle to the province he might well breed his Ngunis with beefier cattle so that he could sell the progeny to feedlots.

Bongi Madlala (not his real name), another beneficiary of the Nguni programme, farms near Utrecht in northern KwaZulu-Natal. Madlala grew up on the farm, where his father was a labourer, but moved to Johannesburg to work as a motor mechanic. A few years later, the white farmer sold the land to Madlala's father. Some time after that, Madlala's father died, leaving the farm to his son.

The white farmer's son later rented a portion of the farm. A fan of Ngunis, it was he who prodded Madlala to apply for the cattle. The application was successful, and Madlala received 30 cattle. Unfortunately, about half of them were bulls:

According to the rules I am not supposed to buy and sell for five years, but I soon saw that that will not work. You cannot have too many bulls in one herd. It causes havoc. So I sold them, not to the auctions where the authorities would find out, but to the abattoirs.

Madlala did not get much money for the bulls, but reckoned that his herd, which now numbers more than 100, was stronger as a result. Among Madlala's concerns were his new neighbours, members of a trust that all lived together on a farm that used to be occupied by just one white commercial farming family:

There are so many of them. They are always feuding and there is so much chaos.

Politicians were also cause for concern:

Politicians come to us black farmers and tell us one thing by day, and they tell the white farmers another thing by night. It is hard to know what to believe. All I trust is my cattle.

By 2018, the IDC had contributed R59.6 million to its Nguni programme since its inception, which has been topped up by provincial government funding in most provinces. But after Mohajane retired in 2015, the IDC's enthusiasm for Ngunis waned. Mohajane has been scouting for new funding sources, which he hopes will allow the programme to expand, both geographically into East Africa, and vertically into beneficiation projects such as abattoirs and tanneries:

Ngunis are the future. They are grass-fed. They are indigenous. In Africa we boast about our 'big five' animals in game parks, but we should add Ngunis and make it the 'big six'.

Mohajane's enthusiasm for Nguni cattle is contagious, and the programme certainly seems more robust than many of the agricultural projects launched in South Africa over the years, if only because it is still going. Land-reform academic Professor Ben Cousins, however, was more sceptical:

The production model behind this Nguni scheme might look innovative, but in reality it is the same as all the others. Commercial farming. Large farms. Fences.

Mohajane disputed this analysis, pointing to the fact that while the scheme's recipients, particularly in Limpopo, included those who had been given commercial farms by the state, it also included co-operatives of poorer people who had pooled their land. And he was unapologetic about the scheme's land requirements:

> You have to have land. You can't keep cattle in the kitchen. And you must have water. We wanted this scheme to work, after all.

An opposing view

Leon Burger, Namibia's Farmers Support Project mentor, described the Sanga – a cousin of the Nguni – as 'the 4×4 of cattle ... tough'. Others beg to differ.

One such person was Freddy Hertzberg, a Namibian livestock trader I met in the magnificently named Otjimbingwe, west of Windhoek, where he instructed me to leave my car and head out with him to the resettlement farms to trawl for cattle to purchase. Hertzberg was a short, stocky man not afraid to speak his mind. He soon made clear his disdain for Ngunis and Sanga:

> I am a cattle speculator. I try to buy cattle that are 380 kilos to 450 kilos. I am not fussy about breeds but I don't want Ngunis and I don't want Sanga. I don't care what people say about them, they are simply not meat cattle. They are just too small. After I've bought cattle, I keep the cattle for 10 to 16 months until I've got them up to around 550 kilos. Then I sell them. I have just sold 900 cattle to Meatco. I have 700 left and I need to buy some more. Tomorrow I will buy 25 cattle, if the price is right.

At one of the farms, Hertzberg pulled up and hailed a farm inhabitant standing nearby. The man, Charles, was a butcher by trade. In 1986,

Charles said, the Walvis Bay butchery where he worked was destroyed in an infamous bomb attack, for which I later learned PW Botha's government blamed the South West Africa People's Organisation (SWAPO) while SWAPO blamed Botha's security forces. The blast killed five people. Hertzberg asked Charles what he thought about Ngunis. Ngunis grew too slowly, Charles replied. He preferred Simbras. The bigger problem, Charles said, was not which breed to have, but grazing:

> Grazing is hard to find. These days, we can walk 15 km to find it. We have no water.

It seemed an odd argument, that grazing is scarce, but we don't like the few breeds that can withstand the drought conditions because they are too lean. And, in fact, it is not Ngunis, but rather the European cattle breeds that commercial farmers love for their high meat content, that are least adapted to the realities of climate breakdown in already-dry Southern Africa. As water becomes scarcer and soil degradation and desertification shrinks available grazing, as the health sciences develop a clearer picture of the consequences of doping feedlotted cattle up with hormones and antibiotics, and as the climate crisis lobby gains traction in its call to eliminate livestock as a methane source, the various links in the commercial cattle supply chain will have no option but to adapt or die. And no cattle breed in this part of the world is better at adapting than the Nguni.

Ngunis at the heart of soil improvement

While the IDC programme uses Ngunis for economic upliftment in rural communities, some farmers are using them to restore the productive capacity of soil. One such farmer is Kevin Watermeyer.

Watermeyer keeps a herd of Ngunis in the foothills of the Sneeuberg Mountains in the Eastern Cape. One crisp, cloudless day in July I drove out to visit his farm – a wide expanse of dry, yellow-green grassland, the snow-flecked mountain slopes beyond visible in the distance. In the early 19th century, the white farmers who came to this land shot all the indigenous fauna so that they could farm sheep, just as the colonial governor Sir Harry Smith always wanted. Sheep continued to dominate the land until Watermeyer, an independent-minded soul, broke with tradition and started farming cattle instead.

When I met him, Watermeyer had a herd of 180 pure Nguni and another commercial herd of 200 mixed-Nguni cattle. He explained his thinking:

> We have to stop thinking that bigger is better and obsessing about the bone-to-meat ratio of our cattle. I take my cue from the natural game of this area. Look at the rheebok, the kudu, the steenbok … they all have compact rumps. It fits with the nutritional inputs we have available to us in this part of the world. Yet South African breeders are breeding cattle with massive rumps. That is the opposite of nature. Ngunis have the same compact frames as game animals. They fit what nature has made available here.

Watermeyer has detected a welcome trend among discerning consumers for smaller portions of better-quality meat – which he reckoned Ngunis are ideally suited to provide. When asked about the aversion of feedlots to Ngunis, Watermeyer replied that he had a similar aversion to feedlots, even though he had no choice but to sell cattle from his mixed herd to them:

> Look, I am a beef farmer, both directly, through my commercial herd, and indirectly, with my Nguni herd via the breeder market. The beef industry in South Africa is dominated by feedlots. I have deep concerns about those feedlots … I don't think we should be feeding grain to cattle, for starters. Then there is their environmental impact … But as an industry we have gone so far down the feedlot route that we can't stop it without a crash. So yes, I do sell to them.

As problematic as feedlots are, what most weighed on Watermeyer's mind was knowing that the Karoo land he farms and loves once teemed with indigenous wild herbivores before it was parcelled up and fenced:

> A hundred and fifty years ago, there were 16 million springbok here! Sixteen million! Imagine that! I doubt we even have half that number of animals on the veld now, in total.

Despite a steep reduction in the number of animals it supports, the soils of the Karoo are steadily degrading. Watermeyer believes this is because the land is fenced. Fencing, he said, is the most radical technology ever to have hit the Karoo, encouraging overgrazing and, ultimately, desertification.

Watermeyer is a follower of the farming philosophy of Zimbabwean ecologist Allan Savory, who famously (and controversially) contends that a grazing practice known as holistic planned grazing (HPG) can reverse the spreading desertification of seasonal grasslands by enabling soil to better absorb and hold rainwater, store carbon and break down methane. The next chapter takes a closer look at the arguments of Savory and others like him and discusses how agricultural grazing practices are undergoing a change that could reverse the world's increasingly dim view of farming cattle.

CHAPTER EIGHT

Farming cattle for the future

Archaeological evidence suggests that it was eating meat that originally gave us the energy we needed to evolve from small-brained *hominins* to big-brained humans, and that the practice has come naturally to us for thousands of years. That said, humans have worked hard since to create a world where we do not have to and indeed do not limit ourselves to what comes 'naturally'. We have electricity so that we don't have to go to sleep when the sun sets and contraception so that we can have pregnancy-free sex. And we have developed such a strong understanding of our bodies' nutritional needs that we can live meat-free lives without suffering any health consequences. For most modern humans, eating meat is a choice – and particularly when it comes to beef, a choice that is under fire.

Vegans and vegetarians have long advocated plant-based diets, but until recently, mainstream society has managed largely to tune out their pleas. What has changed? The big shift is our much-improved understanding of the global environmental consequences of humans eating industrially farmed meat on the scale that we do. Vegans and vegetarians have traditionally made their pitch on the grounds of health and humanity – that plant-based diets are kinder to animals and better for you. But there are respectable counter-arguments to both, even if you personally are not convinced by them, such as that there would be no livestock if we did not eat meat and consume dairy, that many soils need animals on them to thrive, and that meat and dairy are actually good for you. But it is much harder to dispute the climate crisis argument, that you should not consume meat or dairy because their large-scale production is accelerating the effects of climate breakdown, which has the potential to render the planet uninhabitable for everyone.

As is by now pretty well known, when we burn fossil fuels, carbon is released into the atmosphere, in the form of carbon dioxide (CO_2), methane (CH_4) or a range of other molecules. The carbon hangs around, forming a blanket around Earth that allows heat from the sun to enter our atmosphere but stops reflected heat from leaving. This creates an escalating heating cycle commonly known as the greenhouse effect.

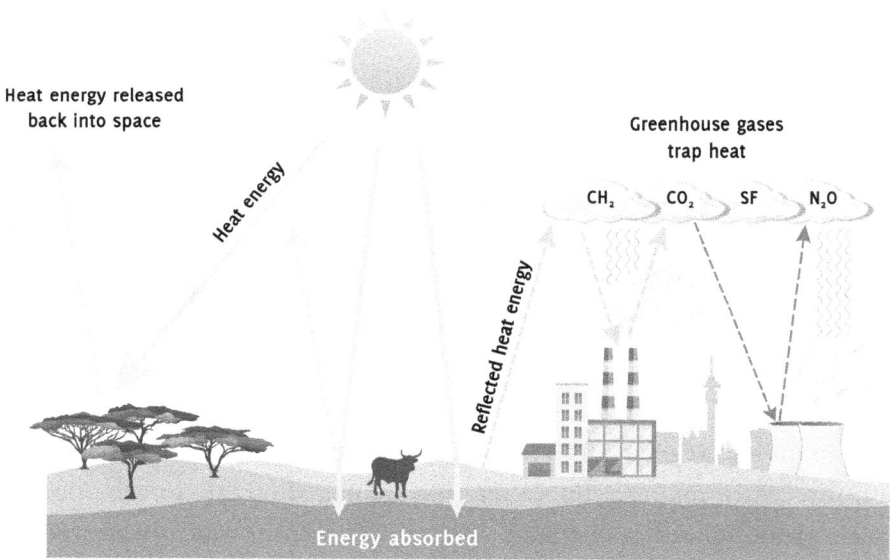

FIGURE 1. *The greenhouse effect*

The climate change, or more accurately the climate crisis case against farming cattle hinges on three separate, but related, claims.

First, poor farming practices and excessive livestock are damaging the soil and killing its ability to grow plants. Fewer plants increases the land's albedo – that is, its heat reflectiveness – so increasing the amount of heat being pumped into, and trapped, in the atmosphere, effectively accelerating global warming, or, as science writers now prefer to call it, global heating.

Second, this soil degradation limits its capacity to act as a carbon sink. According to the United Nations Food and Agriculture Organization (FAO), the world's soil has the potential to sequester 20 petagrams – that is, 20 billion tonnes – of carbon dioxide each year.

Third, the livestock kept to supply global demand for meat produces large volumes of methane, directly exacerbating the greenhouse effect.

This chapter examines these arguments in closer detail to determine whether they mean we need to completely eliminate meat from our diets – or if there is another way.

Does cattle farming really destroy soil health?

Poorly done, cattle farming definitely can destroy soil health – one has only to look at the fetid lagoons of manure in the large American feedlots to appreciate this. But according to Savory, the Zimbabwean ecologist briefly introduced at the end of the last chapter, if cattle farming is properly managed, it can do the exact opposite and instead build soil health and vitality. The question, then, is: what does it mean to properly manage cattle farming?

When seasonal grasses die, Savory says, they must decay biologically (rot, basically) in order to prepare the soil for the next growing season. If the grasses oxidise rather than decompose – that is, if they dry out and become brittle without breaking down into their component organic parts – then they need to be removed or flattened so that new grasses can grow. If this doesn't happen, new grass will not grow and the soil will become bare and exposed. Soil degradation and desertification will follow.

To stop this happening, communities worldwide often burn the dead grasses. This is not particularly effective in restoring the soil, however, and it releases tons of carbon in the process. A better solution, Savory argues, is to use livestock to mimic the behaviour of large herds of wildlife as they trample, urinate and scatter dung all over the dead grass and soil, creating a rich mulch of decomposing organic matter that is able to trap and absorb water, promote future plant growth, and sequester atmospheric carbon within the soil more effectively.

Central to Savory's approach is the idea that grazing in a given area should be intense but short-lived, so that the plants still have enough energy stored in their roots to grow new, tender leaves. Watermeyer described it like this:

> Animals eat all the good stuff within their patch. Then they second bite it. That means those plants lose their root energy and they never get to hang on to their sun energy. Only the plants that the animals do not want to eat retain their sun energy. That changes the fauna. That is why the grazing is getting worse and small farms are going under as a result.

In an ideal world, desertification in areas like the Karoo, where Watermeyer farms, could be slowed or reversed by allowing livestock and wildlife to follow natural migration patterns, unhindered by fences. As it is, the fencing that currently demarcates private property also restricts the animals' movement, encouraging second biting in certain areas and disrupting the Karoo's fragile ecology. To reverse this, Watermeyer has been trying to forge agreements with his immediate neighbours to combine and graze their herds over a much larger area:

> I want to see 1 000 head of cattle on this land, moving in a herd. We aren't anywhere near that yet, but we are getting there. That will generate a lot of trampling and littering. And that is good for the land here, as long as it is only for a limited period. This land is too brittle here to cope with that sort of pressure for long … There are some fencing requirements for that, it is true, but mostly it is about careful herding.

Savory's approach to land management has met multiple challenges, not least from Dr Richard Fynn, a grazing ecosystem ecologist based at the Okavango Guiding School. In an article published in South Africa's

Farmer's Weekly in 2015, Fynn argues that endlessly moving herds around is a poor, effort-intensive way to minimise selective overgrazing. He believes that, to better mimic the grazing habits of wild herbivores, livestock should be allowed to graze and re-graze an area for longer than Savory prescribes, such that both the high-quality grass of the wet season and the low-quality, tall grasses of the dry season get eaten. Once the re-grazing is complete, the soil should be given a year to recover rather than the few days or weeks that Savory recommends.

Fynn's theory is attractive in its simplicity: instead of having multiple fenced-off grazing areas and herding livestock from one field to the next according to a rigorous schedule, Fynn's method requires that a livestock farm be divided into two (or four, if there is more than one herd), with one half being used for grazing while the other recovers. The half being grazed (and re-grazed) would be full of immature, rapidly growing and nutritious grasses, while on the resting half, the grass will grow tall, providing plentiful forage when the cattle move over in the following year's dry season. The result: less work for the farmer, better grass, and, Fynn reckons, increased carbon sequestration.

Curious to learn how Fynn came to his theory, I called him up. Fynn, it transpired, used to be a fan of HPG but changed his mind after moving to Botswana and studying the movement of game for himself. According to Fynn, herbivores don't graze in the tight, ever-moving herd that Savory says they do:

> Herbivores like to spread out, not bunch up. And in the wild, 95% of the time that is exactly what they do. It is true that they come together when there are predators, but that is only a small percentage of the time. And after the predators are gone, they do not move on to new grazing. They go back to the same grazing.

And the trampling and aerating that comes from high-density grazing? Isn't that good for regenerating degraded soil? It is, but tightly clumped herds of ever-moving livestock are not the only way to achieve this.

According to Fynn:

> If you simply concentrate all your animals on one side of your ranch, you will end up getting much bigger trampling without having to move them around and herd them.

What about re-grazing? According to Savory, when plants regrow after being grazed, until they produce leaves for photosynthesis they draw their energy from their roots, and thus from the soil. Re-grazing results in the plant never reaching the stage where it is able to photosynthesise, so the plant essentially draws more from the soil than it would if it were allowed to grow leaves. This depletes the soil and it is to avoid this outcome that HPG prescribes moving cattle around, in order to stop them from re-grazing.

Fynn, however, said Savory has his science wrong:

> Plants' nutrients always come from the soil, not from sunlight. What they get from the sun, from photosynthesis, is carbohydrates. Some of these are stored in the leaves, and some in the roots. And when the plant regrows after grazing, most of the regrowth also comes from photosynthesis – from the sun.

Moreover, said Fynn, re-grazing gives rise to plant regrowth, which is so good for cattle that it is madness for farmers to prevent them from eating it:

> Plant regrowth is very nutritious and digestible. And in the wet season you need that, because cows are conceiving, carrying calves, dropping calves, and producing milk. They need good food. Over-mature grass is less digestible and has fewer proteins but it is okay for the cattle to get by on during the dry season.

Several academic studies support Fynn's position, arguing that short-duration grazing has little discernible impact on soil conditions and that large, dense herds, for all their trampling, do more harm than good because of the soil erosion they cause. Furthermore, higher stocking rates, as advocated by Savory, expose farmers to greater risk if – or, in southern Africa, when – drought strikes.

Fynn compares Savory and his HPG adherents to 'a cult' that has part of the story right, but is quickly offended by criticism, however valid. If HPG worked as well as Savory said it does, Fynn maintains, farmers who practised it should all have wonderful soil and grass, and well-nourished, healthy cattle. Yet, with some honourable exceptions, there was precious little evidence of this to be found.

Does HPG improve soils? Clearly Fynn thought not. Watermeyer, on the other hand, was convinced, believing that herding cattle in this way benefits topsoil in ways we do not yet fully understand:

> We don't know that much about topsoils yet. We know they contain tens of millions of organisms, but most of them we know almost nothing about. But they are surely likely to turn out to be beneficial to the planet.

Watermeyer reached down to scoop up a handful of earth. As we watched his stately Nguni graze nonchalantly nearby, he slowly allowed the dark grains to run through his fingers. Watermeyer said he was unfazed by the welter of criticism Savory has received: 'The soil I see here tells me he is right.'

He is not alone in his faith. In Australia, a company named Sustainable Land Management claims to have doubled cattle-stocking rates on farms in extremely dry areas using HPG, improving plant diversity and reducing dependence on feeds into the bargain. In the United States, Allen Williams, Gabe Brown and Neil Dennis – whose story is told in the 2013 short film, *Soil Carbon Cowboys* – also claim their farms' soil is sequestering more carbon because of HPG.

Closer to home, another farmer who takes his inspiration from Savory is Angus McIntosh – or 'Farmer Angus', as he brands himself – who farms on Spier Estate near Stellenbosch. Spier is best known for its wines, restaurant and theatrical events, but McIntosh has become known as a producer and retailer of pasture-reared meat and eggs.

McIntosh says he first decided to become a farmer after reading about Joel Salatin, a self-styled 'Christian-conservative-libertarian-environmentalist-lunatic farmer' from Virginia who has become something of a legend (in eco-farming circles at least) for his mixed-livestock approach, though Salatin calls himself a grass farmer. Similar to Savory, Salatin focuses not on the animals but what is beneath their feet: in his case, the quality and diversity of the grasses on his farm. Salatin aims to make sure that his pastures are able to nourish the livestock without additional inputs and, through careful management, and again without additional inputs, that the livestock nourishes the pastures.

I visited McIntosh in late 2015. We met in a large farm shed, which housed a long table half-buried under paperwork and open cook books showing recipes for bone broths. Like Salatin, McIntosh keeps both cattle and other livestock, moving the animals around regularly to build soil fertility and improve the farm's grasses. In line with Savory's thinking, McIntosh likes to allow his grass to recover between bouts of grazing. 'We manage the grass so that the cattle hammer it hard on day one, and then they don't come back for another six to eight weeks,' he said. 'We give the grass a proper rest.'

McIntosh keeps Limousin crossbreeds. Limousins are a pleasant golden-red breed that hails, as the name suggests, from Limousin in France. Although he saw the appeal of Nguni cattle for farms where conditions are harsh, the lush, green fields of Spier posed no such challenges, allowing for meatier breeds to be farmed.

Limousin cattle have a good meat-to-bone ratio – that is, there is a lot of meat in relation to bone mass – making them popular with commercial farmers, particularly those that feed their cattle supplements. McIntosh, however, feeds his herd only grass. They also never see the inside of a feedlot: when they reach the right size, he sends them directly to Malmesbury for slaughter, butchering the meat himself on the farm.

McIntosh sells his grass-fed beef at a premium directly to the public and at organic food stores in Cape Town and Stellenbosch. He believes that contact with the customer is an important element of what he does:

> Very few farmers have direct relationships with the consumers. It is always via retailers. And for the retailer, it is not what he is selling that counts to him. The key metric is returns per metre of shelf space. In that paradigm, you do not get true cost accounting. The true cost of production of what is being retailed is not factored in. Because of industrial agriculture and feedlots, we are cutting down forests. Polluting water. Giving people inflammatory diseases because the omega levels in our meat are out of balance. About 90% of the antibiotics in South Africa are fed to animals, and feedlots are a big part of that. But none of that is incorporated in the price the product is retailed for. And it should be. With my operation, there are no hidden costs. All the costs are priced into what I sell for.

Ingeniously, Farmer Angus, who is a former investment banker at Goldman Sachs, has arranged matters such that Spier – the property of billionaire Dick Enthoven, who also owns Nandos and the Hollard insurance group – earns carbon credits from Credible Carbon, which is a South African carbon registry that then sells these credits to companies looking to 'offset' their own pollution. Farmer Angus, meanwhile, claims that Spier's carbon credits make his beef 'carbon negative'.

As tasty as Farmer Angus's meat is, is it not all impossibly niche? How could farming operations like his, producing top-quality products at top-drawer prices, ever be scaled up to meet the nation's food needs, and especially those of the poor? McIntosh admitted that he was not sure, but said he reckoned a good part of the answer was to rip up the country's vast sugar estates and turn them into pasture:

> Just drive down the coast from Durban to Transkei or up to
> Swaziland. All you see is sugarcane. And what does that do? It
> makes humans fat and sick. And it pollutes the earth. But what if
> you replaced it with multi-species pasture? You would sequester
> carbon. You wouldn't poison people and you would get plenty
> of good beef.

The soil quality at Spier and Watermeyer's cattle farm seems to support the idea that well-managed livestock have an important role to play in the creation and maintenance of healthy soil. We also know that healthy soil can sequester carbon, but can it ever sequester enough to justify the global heating impacts of cattle farming?

Can healthy soil really trap enough carbon to reverse global heating?

When herbivores graze, they remove some of the carbon from vegetation, eventually breathing it out as carbon dioxide or in the form of methane burps. However, they also return some to the soil, in the form of dung. Some of this dung carbon gets lost as methane and carbon dioxide but, as dung beetles and the like do their work, the dung slowly becomes incorporated into the soil. This incorporation can take the form of temporary carbon storage or more long-term carbon sequestration.

Simply put, carbon sequestration refers to the process whereby soil, under the right conditions, incorporates some of the carbon in organic matter – things like decomposing plant matter, animal manure and live roots – into the soil as a stable compound, effectively removing it from the atmosphere. Soil-based carbon sequestration is similar but different to soil-based carbon storage, which is when carbon is trapped in soil as upper soil organic matter (see the illustration below) but has not yet been converted to more stable compounds (lower soil organic matter).

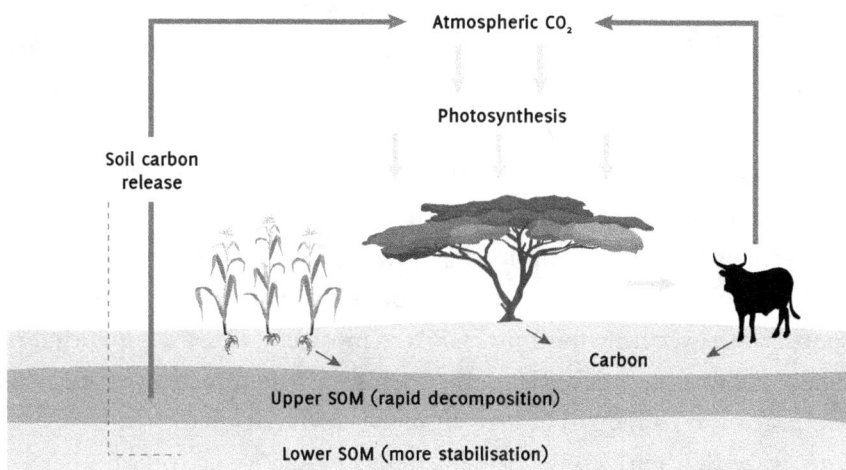

FIGURE 2. *The more stable compounds in the layer of lower soil organic matter (SOM) lie below the upper SOM.*

Provided the soil is not disturbed – as it is in commercial agriculture, for example, when ploughs prepare land for crops – stored carbon can, over time, evolve into more stable, *sequestered* carbon. This conversion process slows and finally comes to a halt when equilibrium is reached, meaning a soil's carbon emissions and removals are in balance with each other.

Grazed and Confused?, a 2017 report by the University of Oxford's Food Climate Research Network (FCRN), provides some insight into the complicated business of how soil and carbon dioxide interact, drawing on research from Britain, the Netherlands, Sweden, Switzerland and Australia – but not, sadly, Africa. In it, the lead authors Tara Garnett and Cécile Godde support Savory's claim that soil is, indeed, a 'very significant' carbon store. Peatlands store the most carbon per hectare of any land type, followed by tropical forests and then grasslands. Savannah, which is much of South Africa, does not fare too badly in this regard either and is estimated to hold about a third of the total global soil carbon stock.

Measuring soil carbon stocks is, however, a tricky business. You need to drill down one metre to retrieve a soil sample for analysis. This sample is then assumed to represent the carbon stocks for the first metre of soil for that area. However, studies show this is often not the case. Carbon sequestration is also difficult to assess because sequestration levels vary markedly over time, with conversion rates peaking during the first few years and then slowing down. Savory boldly uses a steadily upward-pointing linear projection to predict how much carbon soil can sequestrate over time, but the FCRN is more cautious, arguing that it takes 'about a decade' just to get a sense of the direction of carbon sequestration change in any given place, and that even then, one can only trace that with conviction by analysing plenty of soil samples.

One of the main ways herbivores help soil to store and sequester carbon is by eating plant nitrogen when they graze, returning some of it to the soil in the form of dung and urine. Part of this nitrogen runs off, but some of it penetrates the soil, stimulating plant growth and encouraging the organic decomposition of soil organic matter. Grazing animals potentially aid carbon sequestration in another important way too, as their grazing can stimulate growth, both above and below ground. Below the ground, root growth will, if left undisturbed, eventually be converted into a stable form of carbon.

All this bolsters Savory's case, but does not do so conclusively, since at no stage does livestock ever add any *new* carbon or nitrogen into the soil. Rather, as the FCRN argues, livestock 'merely contribute[s] to their accumulation in some compartments (reservoirs) along the cycle: in soils, or in plant and animal biomass'. The word 'merely' seems harsh, since carbon accumulation in the atmosphere is at the heart of the problem, and any mechanism that removes it, even if only temporarily, can still help slow global heating. Nonetheless, it is too often forgotten that soil-based carbon sequestration is not eternal and can quite easily be reversed.

The FCRN and Savory agree that good grazing management and the 'right' animal-stocking methods and rates (which is, as we have seen, much debated) has the potential to maintain the soil's stock of carbon and, in some contexts, boost the sequestering of more. But that is where the agreement ends. Whereas Savory, aided by his linear projection, claims that good livestock management could sequester '500 billion tonnes of carbon over 40 years', which, if true, would return our planet's carbon dioxide levels to those of pre-industrial times, the FCRN strongly disagrees, saying the figure is way too high.

To reach his 500 billion tonnes, Savory makes three principal claims. One is that carbon can be sequestered at a rate of 2.5 tonnes of carbon per hectare per year; the second is that there are 5 billion hectares of grassland available worldwide for livestock to graze on, and the third is that a high carbon sequestration rate can be maintained for at least 40 years. The FCRN dispute all three claims, pointing out that the first two figures are substantially higher than almost anyone else's scientific estimates, and that it is 'vanishingly unlikely' that a high carbon sequestration rate can be maintained for as long as 40 years, since equilibrium would be reached long before then. For good measure, the report's authors also cite evidence that suggests soils sequester more carbon when they are allowed to rewild without any livestock at all.

Savory's claims about the soil's potential to sequester carbon do seem overdone. Even so, there is a general consensus that better livestock management can and does benefit soil health, and can result in carbon sequestration. However, if the FCRN is correct, where carbon sequestration gains are achieved – whether from holistic, wildlife-integrated or no livestock grazing – they will neither be durable nor very large. Further, when compared to the global heating contribution currently made by livestock, soil-based carbon sequestration does not, after all, constitute the climate breakdown silver bullet that holistic grazers claim it to be.

The figures speak for themselves. In 'Soil Carbon Sequestration and Biochar as Negative Emission Technologies', a 2016 paper published in *Global Change Biology*, author Pete Smith estimates that the world's total carbon sequestration potential is 800 megatonnes (a megatonne is a billion kilograms) of carbon dioxide equivalent a year. Smith's is the highest estimate for the soil's carbon sequestration potential in all currently available peer-reviewed journals. Optimistically, Smith further estimates that just more than half of this volume, 53%, could be achieved by changed livestock grazing practices.

Yet even this generous carbon sequestration estimate, as the FCRN point out, is nearly *eight times lower* than the livestock sector's current carbon dioxide equivalent emissions, which stand at seven gigatonnes – 7 000 megatonnes – a year. The FCRN is unequivocal in its assessment:

> Even assuming the maximum mitigation potential [from carbon sequestration], the grazing sector would continue to be a net emitter … If we want to continue to eat animal products at the level we do today, then the livestock sector will continue to be a very significant emitter of greenhouse gases. Grazing management, however good, makes little difference.

And this is without adding any of the extra livestock that Savory is advocating in order for them to trample more soil and boost its sequestration potential. But adding more livestock would inevitably result in methane emissions that climbed even further beyond any potential mitigating carbon sequestration effect their introduction to the landscape might have.

How big a problem is methane from livestock?

When it comes to greenhouse gases, carbon dioxide is the heavy hitter. Carbon dioxide is reckoned to account for 60.3% of all man-made emissions in South Africa, most of which come from burning fossil fuels. By comparison, methane from ruminants accounts for 4% of man-made emissions and methane has an atmospheric lifespan of only 12 years compared to carbon dioxide's 200, which make it seem like a far lesser threat.

These points are argued persuasively in ecologist Simon Fairlie's provocative book, *Meat: A Benign Extravagance*, in which he claims that methane's relatively short atmospheric lifespan means the damage it does is short-lived. Fairlie further pointed out that we need to understand more about methane before taking drastic action like culling livestock, citing 2006 research by the Max Planck Institute that showed that plant tissues can generate methane in the absence of oxygen (as when, for example, they are under water in a swamp), which we already knew, but aerobically too, which we did not. This might explain why strong methane fields have been detected over tropical forests.

Fairlie also pointed to a 2008 study by the UN's FAO which found that, despite an increase in the number of ruminants, atmospheric methane concentrations have levelled off since 1999. Reasonably enough, he concludes that 'the role of ruminants in greenhouse gases may be less significant than originally thought, with other sources and sinks playing a larger role in global methane accounting'.

For a long time, I was persuaded by this argument. But Fairlie spoke too soon. By the time his book was published in 2010, methane emissions had again started increasing year on year – and there is no indication that they will slow down any time soon.

Beyond these fluctuations in emissions, the trouble with methane remains that, gram for gram, it contributes more to global heating than almost any other greenhouse gas. It is true that methane's atmospheric lifespan is only 12 years compared to carbon dioxide's 200, but during that short period methane is a far more dangerous form of carbon. During its first five years in existence, methane traps 100 times more heat than carbon dioxide can over the same period. (In technical terms, methane is said to have a global heating potential that is 25 times that of carbon dioxide. However, global heating potential is assessed over a 100-year period, so the true effect of methane, which is only around for 12 of those years, is, in effect, mathematically diluted.)

And anyway, where there is an endless supply of cattle, all churning out an endless supply of methane, this 12-year atmospheric lifespan becomes an eternity. As the FCRN put it in in *Grazed and Confused?*:

> Although the warming impact of a given tonne of the gas may be transitory, if the source of the gas continues to exist, so do the effects. For a steady rate of methane release – as emitted by a constant number of cattle – the warming effects of a tonne of gas emitted tomorrow replaces the dwindling effects of the tonne of gases emitted today. This means that the warming effect of methane in the atmosphere persists …

In other words, it doesn't matter that one cow's methane emissions do not last long in the atmosphere if these emissions are, upon this cow's death, immediately replaced by another cow's, and another's, and then another's. Or, as the authors put it, 'as long as ruminant livestock production continues, so do methane emissions'.

The FCRN agrees with Fairlie on one point: the 4% versus 60% issue means that there is no point in tackling methane emissions without simultaneously lowering carbon dioxide emissions. The report's authors are right to insist, however, that reducing livestock numbers must still be part of the solution and not shelved to a future time when more progress is made on the carbon dioxide issue, because methane's short lifespan means that its reduced output translates into quicker gains. Were livestock production to stop tomorrow, they say, 'within a few decades the legacy of the methane emissions would disappear also'.

Here in South Africa, my calculation is that the reduction in carbon and methane emissions that would be achieved by culling all the cattle in the country would be cancelled out by just one new energy project: the Medupi coal-fired power station being built in Limpopo. There are roughly 14 million cattle in South Africa, each estimated to generate an average of 95 kilos of methane a year. That makes over 1.3 million tonnes of methane, which is the equivalent of 32.7 million tonnes of carbon dioxide. Once completed (should that day ever come), the Medupi power station is designed to burn 14.6 million tonnes of coal a year, releasing 33.14 million tonnes of carbon dioxide into the atmosphere. This is 500 000 tonnes a year more than the carbon dioxide equivalent of the methane emissions of South Africa's cattle, and will increase the country's total annual emissions by 6.6%.

Many commercial farmers argue that the best way to reduce methane emissions from cattle is to intensify farming, and to extract more production and more value from each cow. For example, Johannes Loubser of Fair Cape, whom we met in Chapter Five, keeps his cattle densely packed in carefully cooled sheds, where he feeds them TMR. He has refined his processes to the point that his cows each produce more than 40 litres of milk a day. Assuming the cows' methane emissions have remained constant over time, Loubser's intensive farming methods yield more dairy per gram of methane emitted than less intensive methods. From a climate breakdown perspective, this seems like good news.

The manager of the Karan Beef feedlot made a comparable case to me, saying that because his cattle are slaughtered at 18 months, they each produce less methane over their short lifetimes than cattle on the veld that are allowed to live twice as long. That argument falls flat, however, when you consider that what feedlotted cows lack in longevity they make up in numbers: each slaughtered animal will soon be replaced by another, so the total number of cattle in feedlots, and the total volume of their methane emissions, remains fairly constant. In a similar way, Fair Cape has not used its cows' greater productivity to reduce their number – and thus their methane emissions – in order to achieve the same volume of milk. Instead, Fair Cape just produces more milk. The FCRN would not be fooled.

Comfortingly for the feedlot industry, there is research showing that grain-fed cattle emit less methane than their grass-fed counterparts, possibly because grass is harder to digest than grain. Even so, it would be a radical overstatement to say that feedlotted cattle are therefore less damaging to our environment than pasture-fed cattle. Missing from such a calculation are the many negative impacts on water and air quality that have been identified at feedlots, and the hefty carbon footprint of the TMR that feedlotted cattle eat, which needs to include the carbon released from soil when land is ploughed to grow crops and transported from field to feedlot. Missing, too, are the health costs to humans of the antibiotics and hormones used to treat and stimulate growth in feedlotted cattle.

Put simply, where intensive cattle farming results in greater numbers of cattle, this is bad news for the atmosphere. Even where farmers are using HPG, and even using generous assumptions about how much carbon soil can sequester with HPG, this would, as we have seen, likely be *entirely cancelled out and more* by the global heating impacts of the methane gas produced by these cattle.

There is one other unexplored alternative for cattle farming that deserves a mention. Several recent studies have found that feeding cattle seaweed supplements can significantly reduce their methane emissions. One Australian study even found that adding a small amount of seaweed to a cow's diet could reduce its methane emissions by an incredible 99%. It sounds too good to be true, and certainly further research is needed to check the findings and to determine whether seaweed supplements are commercially viable, but so far at least the omens are good.

An alternative path

I referred earlier to the FCRN's finding that leaving land to rewild can deliver better carbon sequestration results than farming livestock, even if the farmer uses HPG or the variant proposed by Fynn. But what if you do both, and farm livestock and also rewild? In Namibia, I heard about, but was never able to meet Dr Laurie Marker, a dynamic American who runs the Cheetah Conservation Fund there and is a fervent proponent of this hybrid approach, not only for commercial but also for communal farmers. I later caught up with Marker on the phone, where she explained that it all boils down to biodiversity:

Livestock farmers never like predators. But the real problem is not the predators but their own poor livestock management. Too many farmers still don't realise that they need biodiversity on the land, and predators are part of that biodiversity. Without it, the soil degrades and you end up with even less rain. But here in Namibia, we have shown that it does not have to be this way.

According to Marker, rewilding the land with wildlife alongside livestock boosts diversity in plant growth and appears to generate carbon sequestration gains comparable with, and possibly exceeding, rewilded land without livestock. She spoke enthusiastically about a project in one of Namibia's former homelands, Damaraland, where wildlife conservancies had been successfully integrated with livestock farming:

It reduces poverty, because wildlife brings ecotourism and, on top of that, it brings a good protein source. But it has to be managed properly. That is the key.

I was introduced to Marker by Schneider-Waterberg, the Namibian farmer we first met in Chapter Six, who had contracted her to research community perspectives on development priorities in former Hereroland. According to Schneider-Waterberg, Marker had surveyed 3 000 of the 22 000 people living there during the course of this project. When I asked Marker about her research in Hereroland, she nodded enthusiastically:

It was clear from the research, and anyway we knew already, that people there do indeed love their cattle, and that in addition these cattle are literally the people's bank. You go to the bank when you deposit something or draw something out. Everyone eats when you transfer your cattle into money. Now if cattle are your bank, then you want healthy cattle. You have to learn to vaccinate, to deworm. Livestock management plays a key role.

In Namibia, Marker predicted, subsistence farmers would either continue to get poorer as their land steadily deteriorated, or they could turn things around by shifting towards an integrated system that combines livestock management with wildlife. With wildlife, said Marker, come more and better grasses, which in turn boosted grazing and further encouraged biodiversity. The big challenge in communal areas, she said, was moving towards this new way of keeping livestock:

> We need to find ways to herd cattle for the future. The old ways are too destructive. It means different livestock owners herding their cattle together, and that means changing long, long traditions around trust … who gets to look after your cattle. It is difficult for subsistence farmers to do this on their own. They are too busy surviving. That is where conservationists like me can play a role. I have been doing this for 20 years. In Hereroland in a few years, we could have something to show the world.

Though coming to the subject from a different angle to Savory, Watermeyer, and Farmer Angus, Marker was making the same basic point, which is that well-managed herds of livestock can preserve and restore the land. Beyond that, however, Marker stressed the importance of combining livestock with wildlife management, and argued for a truer pricing mechanism for commercial beef:

> Where livestock management combines with wildlife management, the beneficial effects are huge. And meat consumers should pay a premium for that … Industrial meat is too cheap! The price of the severe ecosystem decline it causes has not been priced into it and it needs to be. And we need better food labelling too, to highlight which farmers have been good stewards of their land.

Marker said she had started off her life in conservation caring just about cheetahs, but as she came to understand the overall picture better, she evolved to becoming first a friend of all nature's predators, and finally to where she is now, passionately in favour of land stewardship. I found it a compelling vision, one that seemed to point the way to a possible sustainable future for South Africa's cattle.

A limited place:
the future of South African cattle

So there it is. For all the immense historical, cultural, spiritual and economic value of cattle and our love for them that this book has been ruminating on, for all the great meat, for all the fine dairy, for all those who live with cattle, and for those who make a living from cattle's slaughter, cattle mean methane, and methane is helping to cook the planet. Is it now time for South Africa to abandon cattle – as well as sheep, horses, and all the other ruminants? Is this book a soliloquy to a culture whose time is up?

For some, the answer is an immediate, resounding yes. The climate crisis vegan position is that what matters is not which livestock farming system is less bad than the other, but that they are all hastening our doom and have to stop. The simple conclusion is that all humans, South Africans included, should stop consuming meat and dairy and stick to entirely plant-based diets instead. That way, livestock production would cease due to lack of demand, so there would be no more methane from cattle and in addition, particularly if land currently under pasture were left to rewild instead, there might be better carbon sequestration too.

But would the overall resulting reduction in the emission of global heating gases be worth the cost? An outrageous question to some perhaps, but if the eradication of the country's livestock were to come without a significant concomitant reduction in the day-in, day-out belching out of carbon emissions from South Africa's industrial economy, and in particular the country's still coal-dominated electricity generation infrastructure, then we would be left bereft of our beloved cattle but with the country's overall global heating profile still more or less unchanged. And that is no good.

For if all livestock were to go, what would that mean to South Africa? Culturally, it would mean the end not just of steak night at Spur, but also of cherished institutions like lobola, and the severing of the spiritual link that cattle provide between families across the generations. Economically, the end of cattle would mean not only a loss of livelihood and income for everyone involved in livestock farming and its long supply and value chains, but it would also herald the end of all the valuable efforts highlighted in this book to use cattle to promote economic upliftment and the rebuilding of the soil.

Life in a post-livestock world

It is important to think through, too, what would be the likely fate of South African soils if our cattle and other livestock were no more. Only 12% of South Africa's land is reckoned to be ideally suited for crops and only 3% is considered 'truly fertile'. Almost all this arable land is already under cultivation. Meanwhile, a full 69% of our land surface is roughly suitable for grazing. What would happen to this grazing land – and our food security – if all livestock were to be removed?

The outcome might conceivably be just as the FCRN suppose: in a post-livestock world, the land currently used to grow crops that are subsequently fed to livestock would be used to grow crops for humans instead, and existing grazing could be allowed to rewild.

This is, to some extent, already happening in places like Namibia, where many commercial farms are being converted into private game reserves. These reserves, however, have been a mixed blessing, winning carbon sequestration gains and, potentially, good money for the landowners, but providing little employment for local and indigenous populations.

While it is true that some of South Africa's grazing would be allowed to rewild in this way, land near urban areas would more likely end up being sold to developers for housing and more shopping malls, exacerbating urban sprawl, which in itself accelerates climate breakdown. And inevitably, some former grazing land would come under the plough.

Crop yields from converted grazing fields, however, are unlikely to match those from suitable cropland and farmers will be tempted to use increasingly high levels of chemical fertilisers, herbicides, insecticides and fungicides to compensate. These products boost crop yields, sometimes dramatically, but they also weaken, and ultimately eliminate, the soil's natural mycorrhizal fungi.

Mycorrhizal fungi maintain soil health through a symbiotic relationship with the roots of plants. Their long, threadlike filaments – called hyphae – carve paths through the topsoil, extending the reach of plants' roots and improving their access to water and nutrients in the soil. In return, the roots provide liquid carbon in the form of a sticky secretion called glomalin, which coats the hyphae. Microbes in the soil feed off this carbon, enabling them to supply minerals to plants in soluble form. The glomalin, meanwhile, binds soil particles, keeping it stable and resistant to erosion. Lose the mycorrhizal fungi and you lose the glomalin, and without glomalin, the soil quickly begins to break up and erode, releasing previously sequestered carbon into the atmosphere.

To make matters worse, the deep ploughing that occurs in commercial crop farming mixes topsoil, which is where mycorrhizal fungi live, with deeper soils that do not contain these fungi. Furthermore, ploughing fields and leaving them without plant cover for prolonged periods reverses soil-based carbon sequestration as carbon in the soil binds with oxygen to create carbon dioxide. And when the sun beats down on bare fields, its energy, instead of being converted into edible biomass like grass, is instead reflected as yet more unwanted heat.

Big vision for a limited place

For all these reasons, phasing out livestock farming in South Africa would not be the straightforward panacea for climate breakdown that some imagine it would be. Even so, the climate breakdown case against commercial livestock farming remains a powerful one. There are fundamental problems with the way cattle are commercially farmed, and much needs urgently to change for the good of the land, the atmosphere and our health.

Commercial farming, though, is not the only way to keep cattle. There are other, less destructive ways to farm livestock, such as those employed by the families living in rural KwaZulu-Natal whom we met in Chapter One, who regard their much-loved cattle partly as economic assets but also as linkages to family members who have passed on. Even if you dismiss their belief system as archaic, the way in which these families keep their cattle is extremely well aligned with contemporary thinking on the least climate-change-inducing way to keep livestock.

To minimise the global heating effect of farming cattle, the cardinal rules are: farm livestock only on land that is unsuited to crop production; feed the cattle only grasses that grow naturally on their grazing land, and if you do offer dietary supplements, use only food waste and by-products from crops produced on the same farm to minimise the need to use fossil fuels to bring in supplements.

As it turns out, most of the land in the former homelands, including where the Gumedes, Mchunus and Ntombelas live, *is* poorly suited to crops. (Indeed, that is one of the reasons why the apartheid government chose those lands – because white commercial farmers had previously rejected them as unsuitable.) And none of their cattle receive much in the way of supplements beyond kitchen scraps.

Does that mean that struggling subsistence rural households, rather than thriving commercial farms, are the rightful future place for cattle in a South Africa committed to slowing climate breakdown? Commercial cattle farmers unhappy with where this argument is going might reasonably ask how then the nation's towns and cities will be fed. After all, two-thirds of South Africans – 37 million people – live in towns and cities. If cattle ownership were to be restricted to rural subsistence households, most urban dwellers would be left without beef or dairy, creating fertile ground for all sorts of rule-breaking, corruption and market distortion.

It is a fair point. An alternative that still helps mitigate the climate breakdown consequences of farming livestock would be for commercial livestock farmers to find creative new ways to farm – more like those employed in rural households – by reducing their herd sizes, restricting their cattle to marginal land unsuited for crops, feeding them only grazing and scraps, and perhaps also using them once more for draught power and manure. It would, I do realise, still be a huge change. The number of the nation's cattle would still plummet, and so would national beef and dairy production, though by less than if livestock production were left to subsistence farmers alone.

It needs to be said upfront that the resulting beef and milk production levels would probably not be enough to meet South Africans' protein needs. According to a recent academic paper, if the whole world farmed livestock only on marginal land and did not supply this livestock with supplements, the agriculture sector would, on average, be able to generate only 21 grams of protein per person per day. That 21 grams would come from either 100 grams of meat and no milk, or 50 grams of meat and 300 millilitres of milk. Because of the legendary capacity of pigs to convert food scraps into protein, most of that meat would be pork. If we exclude pigs, however, the study reckons that the global livestock sector would be able to produce only 12 grams of protein per person per day on average – the equivalent of 25 grams of meat and 150 millilitres of milk per person per day. That is enough to meet only a small fraction of our protein needs, with men requiring roughly

55 grams of protein a day and women 45 grams.

That means that the only way this approach to commercially farming cattle could work is if domestic demand for meat and dairy fell. South Africans would have to choose to eat less beef, drink less milk and source more protein from plants instead. Such a diet may sound grim to some, unpatriotic even, but it has strong roots in history. The country's traditional rural diets do not typically feature a daily dose of red meat. Far from it. Back in the day, cattle were slaughtered only on special occasions. The daily diet was mostly plant-based, sporadically supplemented by meat from chicken and goat, sheep or pig. Game animals, too, if they were to be found.

Could urban South Africans learn to live on, and even like, a diet like that? Could townsfolk live on old-school samp and beans, veggie burgers and pulses, mixed perhaps with some new-school organic quinoa, tofu, soy and almond milk, according to budget and taste? Could they learn to regard some genuinely free-range chicken and eggs as a rare treat, with beef, lamb or goat meat only eaten, down to every edible morsel, at ceremonies and family celebrations? Or is it all too little, too late, and we might as well eat beef, drink milk and be merry, for tomorrow we shall die?

I hope not. Though the hour is plainly very late, as one element in our panoply of efforts to slow down the heating of the planet, surely we can learn to live with much less meat and dairy, and we can be more courageous in our cuts when we do eat meat. In buying and consuming less and better meat and dairy, we can make it clear to livestock farmers and everyone in the beef and dairy value chains that the environmental and health damage caused by current cattle-farming practice needs to end. Commercial livestock farmers need to find ways to extricate themselves from feedlots and keep fewer cattle, and only on land not suited to crops. Those cattle need to be given only water, grazing and agricultural waste, not hormones and antibiotics. And wherever possible, no inputs that need transporting to the farm using fossil fuels should be used.

154

So far, for the most part, this is precisely what is not happening. Yes, some livestock farmers are working hard to restore the health of their soil, and some wealthy consumers have developed a taste for grass-fed beef. But feedlots that fatten up cattle on maize by-products and stimulants still dominate the beef industry, and supermarkets still overwhelmingly prefer to stock a limited range of mostly prime cuts, all from feedlotted, not grass-fed, beef. The dairy sector, meanwhile, is controlled by a handful of mega-operations that keep growing and finding disturbing new ways to make their cows produce more milk, with emerging and smaller-scale farmers increasingly unable to compete. On the consumer side, South Africans faced with steadily rising meat prices have sought to maintain the volume of meat they consume, often sacrificing quality and nutritional value in the process, rather than eating less meat and getting more of their protein from plants.

That cannot be right. We need to move in a different direction, away from excess and towards the country's older, wiser ways of understanding the relationship between us and cattle, even if we do not embrace its ancestral aspects. Cattle can remain wanted and treasured, but less as commodities from which the maximum value must be extracted for the minimum cost, and more as living assets, kept in modest numbers on land where crops will not thrive, whose beef is eaten rarely and when it is, is savoured as a special occasion.

I am sure our ancestors and future generations would approve.

ACRONYMS

ANC	African National Congress
BST	Bovine somatotropin
EFF	Economic Freedom Fighters
FCRN	Food Climate Research Network
FDA	Food and Drug Administration
FAO	Food and Agriculture Organization
HPG	holistic planned grazing
IDC	Industrial Development Corporation
LFTB	lean finely textured beef
Meatco	Meat Corporation of Namibia
NDP	National Development Plan
PLAAS	Institute for Poverty, Land and Agrarian Studies
SAMIC	South Africa Meat Industry Company
TMR	total mix ration
USDA	United States Department of Agriculture
WHO	World Health Organization

SOURCES

Rather than clutter up the book's text with endless footnotes, instead I have listed below, by chapter, the main works I refer to in the text plus some others that either influenced my thinking or supplied me with useful information.

INTRODUCTION
Braai nation under attack

De Fay, S. & Hersov, J. (2006). *Heaven's Herds.* This stunning documentary can be watched at: https://vimeo.com/166656192

Monbiot, G. (2017). 'Goodbye – and good riddance – to livestock farming'. *The Guardian.* 4 October. Available at: https://www.theguardian.com/commentisfree/2017/oct/04/livestock-farming-artificial-meat-industry-animals

Monbiot, G. (2018). 'The best way to save the planet? Drop the meat and dairy'. *The Guardian.* 8 June. Available at: https://www.theguardian.com/commentisfree/2018/jun/08/save-planet-meat-dairy-livestock-food-free-range-steak

CHAPTER ONE
Cattle in South African history

The section on the San, the Khoekhoe and the first arrival of cattle to South Africa was mostly informed by the following sources:

Barnard, A. (1992). *Hunters and Herders of Southern Africa: A Comparative Ethnography of the Khoisan Peoples.* Cambridge Studies in Social and Cultural Anthropology. Cambridge University Press: Cambridge.

Boonzaier, E., Malherbe, C., Berens, P. & Smith, A. (1996). *The Cape Herders: A History of the Khoikhoi of Southern Africa.*

David Philip: Cape Town & Johannesburg.

Ehret, C. (1967). 'Cattle keeping and milking in eastern and southern African history: the linguistic evidence'. *Journal of African History* 8: 1–17.

Kinahan, J. (2000). *Cattle for Beads: The Archaeology of Historical Contact and Trade on the Namib Coast*. Department of Archaeology & Ancient History, University of Uppsala, Sweden; Namibia Archaeological Trust, Windhoek.

Orton, J. (2013). 'An early date for cattle from Namaqualand, South Africa: implications for the origins of herding in southern Africa'. *Antiquity* 87(335): 108–120.

Sadr, K. (2015). 'Livestock first reached southern Africa in two separate events'. *Plos One* 10(1). DOI: 10.1371/journal.pone.0134215

The section which features the first encounter of the Khoekhoe and Portuguese sailors, is largely drawn from the wonderful, and epic:

Mostert, N. (1992). *Frontiers: The Epic of South Africa's Creation and the Tragedy of the Xhosa People*. Jonathan Cape: London.

One of the few published works about the Swellendam cattle killing of 1788 is:

Viljoen, R.S. (1997). *Making Sense of the Khoikhoi Cattle-Killing of 1788: An Episode of Millenarianism in Khoikhoi Society*. University of the Western Cape, Institute of Historical Research: Cape Town.

The 19th century cattle killing called for by Nongqawuse is more well known. The best history of the tragedy is:

Peires, J.B. (1989). *The Dead Will Arise: Nongqawuse and the Great Xhosa Cattle-Killing Movement of 1856–7*. James Currey: London; Ravan Press: Johannesburg; Indiana University Press: Bloomington and Indianapolis.

Also insightful is:

Bradford, H. (2007). 'Not a Nongqawuse story: An anti-heroine in historical perspective'. In N. Gasa (ed.) *Women in South African History*. HSRC Press: Cape Town.

Also riveting are the novels:

Mda, Z. (2006). *The Heart of Redness*. Farrar, Straus & Giroux: New York.

Ntabeni, M. (2018). *Broken River Tent*. BlackBird Books: Auckland Park, Johannesburg.

The following section of the chapter looks at rinderpest and East Coast Fever, about which these studies shed useful light:

Ballard, C. (1986). 'The repercussions of rinderpest: cattle, plague, and peasant decline in colonial Natal'. *International Journal of African Historical Studies* 19: 421–450.

Cranefield, P. (1991). *Science and Empire: East Coast Fever in Rhodesia and Transvaal*. Cambridge University Press: Cambridge.

Phoofolo, P. (1993). 'Epidemics and revolutions: the rinderpest epidemic in late nineteenth-century southern Africa'. *Past & Present* 138: 112–143.

Van Onselen, C. (1972). 'Reactions to rinderpest in southern Africa, 1896–97'. *Journal of African History* 13(3): 473–488.

The final section of the chapter, about tightening government control over black farmers during the 20th century, and these farmers' resistance, required wide reading, but the following works stand out:

Beinart, W. (1994). *Twentieth Century South Africa*. Oxford University Press: Oxford & Cape Town.

Bosman, A.M. (1932). *Cattle Farming in South Africa*. Central News Agency: Johannesburg.

Brownlee, F. (2007). *Ntsukumbini, Cattle Thief*. Penguin: London.

Bundy, C. (1988). *The Rise and Fall of the South African Peasantry*. David Philip: Cape Town & Johannesburg.

Crais, C. (1992*). White Supremacy and Black Resistance in Pre-Industrial South Africa: The Making of the Colonial Order in the Eastern Cape 1770–1865*. Cambridge University Press: Cambridge.

Delius, P. (1990). *Dikgomo Di Ile (The Cattle Have Gone): The Changing Context of Resistance in Sekhukhuneland, 1950–1986*. University of the Witwatersrand, History Workshop: Johannesburg.

Milton, S. (1994). *The Killing Floor: The First World War and the Emergence of the South African Beef Industry 1902–24*. School of African Studies: London.

Mopeli-Paulus, A.S. (2008). *The World and the Cattle*. Penguin: Johannesburg.

Mpe, M. (2004). *Mmadihlofa: The Cow That Produces Delicious and Nutritious Milk in Abundance*. umSinsi Press: Malvern, South Africa.

Opland, J. (1983). *Xhosa Oral Poetry: Aspects of a Black South African Tradition*. Cambridge University Press: Cambridge.

Plaatje, S. (1991, first published in 1916). *Native Life in South Africa, Before and Since the European War and the Boer Rebellion*. Ohio University Press: Ohio.

Rath, S. (1998). *The Complete Cow*. Voyageur Press: Stillwater.

Terreblanche, S. (2002). *A History of Inequality in South Africa 1652–2002*, University of Natal Press: Pietermaritzburg.

CHAPTER TWO

They bring us together: cattle in our homes and lives

This chapter is largely based on fieldwork in northern KwaZulu-Natal, though the names for cattle, and the identification of which parts of the animal different members of the household should eat both come from:

Nyembezi, S. & Nxumalo, O.E.H. (1966). *Inqolobane Yesizwe.* Shuter & Shuter: Pietermaritzburg, Cape Town, Randburg.

The latter part of the chapter references:

Guy, J. (2013). 'Colonial transformations and the home'. In M. Healy-Clancy & J. Hickel (eds) *Ekhaya: The Politics of Home in KwaZulu-Natal.* UKZN Press: Durban.

Ramaphosa, C. & Naudé, D. (2017). *Cattle of the Ages.* Jacana: Johannesburg.

Also significant in shaping my thoughts on the role of cattle in African culture are:

Mtetwa, R.M.G. (1978). 'Myth or reality: the 'cattle complex' in South East Africa, with special reference to Rhodesia'. *Zambezia* 6(1): 23–36.

Schmidt, M.I. (1992). 'The relationship between cattle and savings: a cattle owner perspective'. *Development Southern Africa* 9(4): 433–444.

Sichone, O. (1995). *Grass, Money, and Cattle: The Livestock Dealers of Phalaborwa.* University of the Witwatersrand, Institute for Advanced Social Research: Johannesburg.

Web, C. de B. & Wright, J.B. (eds) (1987). *A Zulu King Speaks: Statements made by Ceshwayo kaMpande on the History and Customs of his People.* University of Natal Press: Pietermaritzburg, and Killie Campbell Africana Library: Durban.

CHAPTER THREE
Tucking in: the culture of eating beef

The quote from Simon Fairlie featured at the beginning of the chapter is from this thought-provoking book:

Fairlie, S. (2010). *Meat: A Benign Extravagance,* Chelsea Green Publishing: White River Junction.

There is a superb and relatively recent edition of Louis Leipoldt's work at:

Leipoldt, L. (2004). *Leipoldt's Food and Wine*. Stonewall Books: Cape Town.

Antjie Krog writes about wors in:

Krog, A. (2008). *Country of My Skull*. Penguin Random House: Johannesburg.

For details of the LFTB patent I refer to, see:

Justia Patents, *Patents by Inventor Anthony J. M. Garwood: Method of separating meat components via centrifuge,* filed June 11, 2012, date of patent April 24, 2018. Available at: https://patents.justia.com/inventor/anthony-j-m-garwood

Useful reads on obesity, malnutrition and food waste in South Africa include:

Joubert, L. (2012). *The Hungry Season*. Picador Africa: Johannesburg.
News24 (2011). 'SA – 3rd fattest country'. News24.com. 14 November. Available at: https://www.news24.com/MyNews24/SA-3rd-fattest-country-20111113

The research this article was based on was later disputed:

Wilkinson, K. (2018). 'Is SA the "fattest nation" in sub-Saharan Africa, with a third of people obese?'. *Africa Check*. 12 February. Available at: https://africacheck.org/reports/is-sa-the-fattest-nation-in-sub-saharan-africa-with-a-third-of-people-obese/

The report found that the original article exaggerated, and that probably 'only' a quarter of South Africans were obese.

Oxfam (2014). *Hidden Hunger in South Africa: The Faces of Hunger and Malnutrition in a Food-Secure Nation*. Oxfam: Oxford.

Sartorius B., Veerman L.J., Manyema M., Chola L. & Hofman K. (2015). 'Determinants of obesity and associated population attributability, South Africa: empirical evidence from a national panel survey, 2008–2012'. *PloS One* 10(6). DOI: 10.1371/journal.pone.0130218

Smith, D. (2010). 'South Africans among world's fattest people, survey finds'. *The Guardian*. 9 September. Available at: https://www.theguardian.com/world/2010/sep/09/south-africa-obesity-survey-health

The Slow Meat Festival does not, unfortunately, do a wonderful job of advertising itself. For a media report on one of its events, see:

Ho, U. (2016). 'One Nguni cow turned into 400 plates of food to teach responsible eating'. *Sunday Times*. 16 September. Available at: https://www.timeslive.co.za/sunday-times/lifestyle/2016-09-18-one-nguni-cow-turned-into-400-plates-of-food-to-teach-responsible-eating/

For a good introduction to the Banting diet, see:

Noakes, T., Creed, S. & Proudfoot, J. (2016). *The Real Meal Revolution: The Radical, Sustainable Approach to Healthy Eating*. Little, Brown: Boston.

For a media report on Noakes' triumph against the Health Professions Council of South Africa (HPCSA), see:

News 24 (2018). *'Noakes clears final hurdle – not guilty says HPCSA Appeal Committee'*. *News 24.com*. 9 June. Available at: https://www.news24.com/SouthAfrica/News/noakes-clears-final-hurdle-not-guilty-says-hpcsa-appeal-committee-20180609

The National Braai Day page I refer to can be found at:

http://braai.com/national-braai-day-mission/

The Herman Wasserman blog about National Braai Day that I quote from can be found in its entirety at:

Wasserman, H. (2013). 'Some of my best friends are braaiers'. *Africasacountry.com*. 25 September. Available at: https://africasacountry.com/2013/09/some-of-my-best-friends-are-braaiers

You can watch the video filmed by another customer of the altercation between Nico Viljoen and Lebohang Mabuya in a Johannesburg Spur at: https://www.youtube.com/watch?v=t39C6VuhlEc

Also useful in informing my thinking for this chapter were:

Buford, B. (2007). *Heat: An Amateur's Adventures as a Kitchen Slave*. Vintage Books: London.

Rimas, A. & Fraser, E. (2008). *Beef: How Milk, Meat and Muscle Shaped the World*. Mainstream: Edinburgh and London.

Schlosser, E. (2002). *Fast Food Nation: What the All-American Meal is Doing to the World*. Penguin: London.

Statistics SA (2017). *Community Survey 2016, Agricultural Households*, Statistics SA: Pretoria.

CHAPTER FOUR
You need to maximise: the economics of industrial beef

The information cited in the section about Karan Beef from the US Department of Agriculture about its grading system comes from:

US Department of Agriculture, Food Safety and Inspection Service (2018). *Inspection and Grading of Meat and Poultry: What Are The Differences?* USDA: Washington. Available at: https://www.fsis.usda.gov/wps/portal/fsis/topics/food-safety-education/get-answers/food-safety-fact-sheets/production-and-inspection/inspection-and-grading-of-meat-and-poultry-what-are-the-differences_/inspection-and-grading-differences

The information about grading meat in South Africa was sourced from:

Department of Agriculture, Forestry and Fisheries (2015)
  Agricultural Product Standards Act, 1990 (Act No. 119 of 1990).
  20 January. Government Printer: Pretoria. Available at:
  https://www.greengazette.co.za/acts/
  agricultural-product-standards-act_1990-119

The best books I have found about the grim realities of industrial farming in the US are:

Foer, J.S. (2009). *Eating Animals*. Penguin: London.
Pollan, M. (2006). *The Omnivore's Dilemma, The Search for a Perfect Meal in a Fast-Food World*. Bloomsbury: London & Berlin.
Schatzker, M. (2010). *One Man's Search for the World's Tastiest Piece of Beef*. Penguin Books: London and New York.

The data I present on how much grassland there is in South Africa comes from the UN's Food and Agriculture Organisation (FAO):

Palmer, A. & Ainslie, A. (2005). 'Grasslands of South Africa'. In J.M. Suttie (ed.) *Grasslands of the World*. FAO: Rome. Available at:
  http://www.fao.org/tempref/docrep/fao/008/y8344e/y8344e03.pdf

Information about agricultural marketing boards during South Africa's National Party era came mainly from historical sources cited in Chapter One.

This book describes in detail something I only allude to briefly in the text, about one woman's attempt to introduce more compassion to the abattoir:

Grandin, T. (2005). *Animals in Translation*. Scribner: New York.

You can find data about trends in South Africa's beef and poultry sales from the Global Agricultural Information Network (GAIN) of the US Department of Agriculture:

Esterhuizen, D. (2015). *The South African Meat Market. GAIN: Pretoria.* Available at: https://gain.fas.usda.gov/Recent%20GAIN%20Publications/The%20South%20African%20meat%20market_Pretoria_South%20Africa%20-%20Republic%20of_9-15-2015.pdf

In addition, Agri Benchmark (www.agribenchmark.org), and the Bureau for Food and Agricultural Policy (www.bfap.co.za) regularly publish reports that provide reams of information and estimates about the global and South African livestock sector.

CHAPTER FIVE
Milking it: the relentless growth of dairy

The information for the opening section, about the country's 2017 butter shortage, came from media reports. The theory that the Banting diet was partly responsible can be found, for example, at:

ENCA (2017). 'Banting, Cape drought contribute to butter shortage in SA'. ENCA. 11 July. Available at: https://www.enca.com/south-africa/banting-cape-drought-contribute-to-butter-shortage-in-sa

The study I cite about dairy farming in the Western Cape can be found at:

Gertenbach, W. (2007). *Dairy Farming in South Africa, Where to Now?* FAO: Rome. Available at: http://www.fao.org/fileadmin/templates/est/COMM_MARKETS_MONITORING/Dairy/Documents/18_William_Gertenbach__paper.pdf

For a blow-by-blow account of the Estina scandal, see:

amaBhungane & Scorpio (2017). '#GuptaLeaks: Despite denials, Free State dairy farm was huge cash spinner for Guptas'. 5 June. Available at: https://amabhungane.org/stories/guptaleaks-despite-denials-free-state-dairy-farm-was-huge-cash-spinner-for-guptas/

Other works that I found particularly helpful for this chapter were:

Botha, M. (2011). *Dairy Sustainability: Ten Environmental Considerations:* World Wildlife Fund. Available at: http://awsassets.wwf.org.za/downloads/dairy_brochure_03.pdf

Kirsten, J. (2007). *The Impact of Market Power and Dominance of Supermarkets on Agricultural Producers in South Africa.* National Agricultural Marketing Council: Pretoria.

Richardson, F.D. (1994). *Models for the Selection of Cow Types for Extensive Meat and Milk Production in Developing Areas.* Overseas Development Institute: London.

Von Bormann, T. (2011). *Life Cycle Assessment of Milk Production in the Western Cape.* Green House: Cape Town.

CHAPTER SIX
Space to graze: cattle and the land question

The literature on land reform in South Africa is vast, and growing. Below is a selection of the works I read on and around the topic while researching this chapter:

Ainslie, A. (ed.) (2002). *Cattle Ownership and Production in the Communal Areas of the Eastern Cape, South Africa.* Research Report No. 10. PLAAS, University of the Western Cape: Cape Town.

Bosman, F. (2007). *Land Reform: A Contextual Analysis.* FW de Klerk Foundation: Cape Town.

Cousins, B. (1996). 'Livestock production and common property struggles in South Africa's agrarian reform'. *The Journal of Peasant Studies* 23(2/3): 166–208.

Cousins, B. & Hebinck, P. (eds) (2013). *In the Shadow of Policy: Everyday Practices in South African Land and Agrarian Reform.* Wits University Press: Johannesburg.

Cousins, B. (2015). 'Through a glass, darkly: towards agrarian reform in South Africa'. In B. Cousins & C. Walker (eds) *Land Divided, Land Restored: Land Reform in South Africa for the 21st Century.* Jacana: Johannesburg.

Dzimba, J. (2005). *Stock Theft and Human Security: A Case Study of Lesotho.* Institute for Security Studies: Pretoria.

Mahanjana, A. (2012). *African Farmers' Association of South Africa's (AFASA) Contribution to the ANC Policy Conference on Land Reform.* AFASA: Centurion.

Mandela, N. (1994). *Long Walk to Freedom.* Macdonald Purnell: Randburg.

Plaut, M. & Holden, P. (2012). *Who Rules South Africa: Pulling the Strings in the Battle for Power.* Jonathan Ball: Johannesburg & Cape Town.

Pringle, E. (2013). 'Land reform and white ownership of agricultural land in South Africa'. *Journal of the Helen Suzman Foundation* 70: 37–42.

Shackleton, S., Shackleton, C. & Cousins, B. (2000). 'Re-valuing the communal lands of southern Africa: New understandings of rural livelihoods'. *Natural Resource Perspectives* 62. PLAAS, University of the Western Cape: Cape Town.

Steinberg, J. (2002). *Midlands.* Jonathan Ball: Johannesburg & Cape Town.

Various Authors. (1999). *At the Crossroads: Land and Agrarian Reform in South Africa into the 21st Century.* Papers from a conference held at Alpha Training Centre, Broederstroom, Pretoria, 26–28 July. PLAAS, University of the Western Cape: Cape Town.

Visser, M. & Ferrer, S. (2015). *Farm Workers' Living and Working Conditions in South Africa: Key Trends, Emergent Issues, and Underlying and Structural Problems.* International Labour Organization: Pretoria.

The article I refer to by Gizaw Negussie can be found at:

Negussie, G. (2015). 'Education for cattle producers – a successful mentorship programme in Namibia'. *Agri Benchmark,* 14 January. Available at: http://www.agribenchmark.org/agri-benchmark/did-you-know/ einzelansicht/artikel//education-fo.html

In addition, the following book provided fascinating insights about 'traditional' pastoralism in Namibia:

Bollig, M. & Gewald, J.B. (eds) (2000). *People, Cattle and Land : Transformations of a Pastoral Society in Southwestern Africa.* Rudiger Köppe: Cologne.

CHAPTER SEVEN
Ngunis and new cow economics

The following is a fair summary of the scientific data on Ngunis:

Erasmus, J.A. (2005). 'The Nguni: pinnacle of an adapted breed?'. *Nguni Cattle Breeders' Society Journal* 2005: 19–25. Available at: http://www.ngunicattle.info/Publications/Journals/2005/ PINNACLE%20OF%20AN%20ADAPTED%20BREED.pdf

This book is a remarkable mix of history, anthropology and art, all dedicated to the Nguni:

Poland, M., Hammond-Tooke, D. & Voight, L. (2003). *The Abundant Herds: A Celebration of the Nguni Cattle of the Zulu People.* Fernwood Press: Vlaeberg.

While this is an evocative novel by one of the authors on the same theme:

Poland, M. (2004). *Recessional for Grace*. Penguin: Johannesburg,

CHAPTER EIGHT
Farming cattle for the future

The following works outline in more detail the debates on grazing and carbon sequestration explored in the chapter:

Food Climate Research Network (2017). *Grazed and Confused? Ruminating on Cattle, Grazing Systems, Methane, Nitrous Oxide, the Soil Carbon Sequestration Question – and what it all means for Greenhouse Gas Emissions*. FCRN: Oxford.

Fynn, R. (2015). 'Towards optimal rangeland management'. *Farmer's Weekly* 14 October. Available at: https://www.farmersweekly.co.za/animals/cattle/ towards-optimal-rangeland-management/

Gammon, D. (1978). 'A review of experiments comparing systems of grazing management on natural pastures'. *Proceedings of the Annual Congresses of the Grassland Society of Southern Africa* 13(1): 75–82.

Savory, A. (2013). 'How to green the world's deserts and reverse climate change'. *TED Talks*. Watch it here: https://www.ted. com/talks/allan_savory_how_to_green_the_world_s_deserts_ and_reverse_climate_change

Scoones, I. (ed.) (1995). *Living with Uncertainty: New Directions in Pastoral Development in Africa*. International Institute for Environment and Development: London.

Skovlin, J. (1987). 'Southern Africa's experience with intensive short duration grazing'. *Rangelands 9(4): 162–167.*

Zacharias, P. (1995). 'Blaze 'n graze: management of sourveld after the burn'. Grassland Society of South Africa 6(2): 12–18.

The 2013 film I refer to about American 'soil carbon cowboys' can be found at: https://vimeo.com/80518559

Massey, C. (2018). *Call of the Reed Warbler: A New Agriculture – a New Earth*. Chelsea Green Publishing: White River Junction.

In addition to the FCRN study *Grazed and Confused?*, these books and articles also helped shape my thinking on cattle, methane and climate breakdown:

Hambin, J. (2017). 'If everyone ate beans instead of beef'. *The Atlantic*. 2 August. Available at:
 https://www.theatlantic.com/health/archive/2017/08/
 if-everyone-ate-beans-instead-of-beef/535536/
Herrero, M., Havlik, P., Valin, H., Notenbaeert, A. et al. (2013). 'Biomass use, production, feed efficiencies, and greenhouse gas emissions from global livestock systems'. *Proceedings of the National Academy of Sciences of the United States of America* (PNAS) 110(52): 20888–20893. Available at:
 http://www.pnas.org/cgi/doi/10.1073/pnas.1308149110
Kesteven, S. (2016). 'Feeding cows seaweed could slash global greenhouse gas emissions, researchers say'. *ABC News*, North Queensland. 20 October. Available at:
 http://www.abc.net.au/news/2016-10-19/
 environmental-concerns-cows-eating-seaweed/7946630
McWilliams, J. (2013). 'All sizzle and no steak: why Allan Savory's TED talk about how cattle can reverse global warming is dead wrong'. *Slate*. 22 April. Available at:
 http://www.slate.com/articles/life/food/2013/04/allan_savory_s_
 ted_talk_is_wrong_and_the_benefits_of_holistic_grazing_have.
 html
Scarborough, P., Appleby, P.N., Mizdrak, A., Briggs, A.D.M. et al. (2013). *Dietary Greenhouse Gas Emissions of Meat-Eaters, Fish-Eaters, Vegetarians and Vegans in the UK*. Nuffield Department of Population Health, University of Oxford: Oxford.

Schwartz, J. (2013). *Cows Save the Planet and other Improbable Ways of Restoring Soil to Heal the Earth*. Chelsea Green Publishing: White River Junction.

Seo, S. (2007). *Climate Change Impacts on Animal Husbandry in Africa: A Ricardian Analysis*. World Bank: Washington.

Smith, P. (2016). 'Soil carbon sequestration and biochar as negative emission technologies.' *Global Change Biology* 22(3):1315–1324. Available at: https://doi.org/10.1111/gcb.1317

United Nations Conference on Trade and Development (UNCTAD). (2013). *Wake Up Before It Is Too Late: Make Agriculture Truly Sustainable Now for Food Security in a Changing Climate*. UNCTAD: Geneva.

Weber, K. (ed.) (2009). Food Inc.: *A Participant Guide: How Industrial Food is Making Us Sicker, Fatter, and Poorer – And What You Can Do About It*. Participant Media: Beverley Hills.

You can find more information about Dr Laurie Marker's Cheetah Conservation Fund at: https://cheetah.org/about-us/message-from-dr-laurie/

INDEX

ABOUT THE AUTHOR

Gregory Mthembu-Salter is a journalist, researcher and writer, specialising in Africa's political economy. He moved from the UK to South Africa in the mid-1990s and lives in Scarborough on the Cape peninsula. As a journalist, he has written for the *Mail & Guardian*, *The Africa Report* and specialist African politics and economics publications. He has served as a member of the United Nations Group of Experts on the Democratic Republic of Congo, appointed by the UN Security Council, and has conducted research there and in South Africa for numerous organisations, including the World Bank, the Organisation for Economic Co-operation and Development, the UK government, non-governmental organisations, and research institutes. He is a research associate of the South African Institute for International Affairs. In the UK, he established and DJ'd at a club in Bristol for several years and continues to DJ from time to time. He is married with three alarmingly grown-up sons. This is his first book.

Lindiwe and Gregory Mthembu-Salter, 2019

ACKNOWLEDGEMENTS

This book has only been possible with the assistance of many, many people who have given generously of their time and knowledge. Sincere thanks to you all. I am particularly grateful to the Mchunu, Gumede and Ntombela families for welcoming me into their homes, and to Tom Ntombela for taking me to them.

A big thank you too to my editors Jennifer Stastny and Mandi Smallhorne, to Angela Briggs who took the book through production, and to Palesa Morudu and the rest of the team at Cover2Cover for believing in this project and for seeing it patiently through to its conclusion.

All errors and omissions are nonetheless my own. The former we have done our best to spot and to remove but the latter are inevitable – indeed this project still feels more like the first than the last word on the subject.

A special thank-you to my family for putting up with this project for over a decade, and especially to Lindiwe for accompanying me on research trips, translating, coming up with good ideas and, above all, for the compassion and solidarity.

www.ingramcontent.com/pod-product-compliance
Lightning Source LLC
Chambersburg PA
CBHW052007270326
41929CB00015B/2827